ST ANDREWS

A HISTORY AND CELEBRATION OF THE TOWN

SHELAGH YOUNG

Produced by The Francis Frith Collection
exclusively for

OTTAKAR'S

www.ottakars.co.uk

First published in the United Kingdom in 2005
by The Francis Frith Collection®

Hardback Edition 2005
ISBN 1-84567-753-6

British Library Cataloguing in Publication Data

St Andrews - A History and Celebration of the Town
Shelagh Young

The Francis Frith Collection
Frith's Barn, Teffont,
Salisbury, Wiltshire SP3 5QP
Tel: +44 (0) 1722 716 376
Email: info@francisfrith.co.uk
www.francisfrith.co.uk

Printed and bound in England

Front Cover: **ST ANDREWS, SOUTH STREET, QUEEN ELIZABETH'S VISIT 1950** SA000385t
(Courtesy of University of St Andrews Library)

Additional modern photographs by Shelagh Young.

The author and publisher gratefully acknowledge the assistance of St Andrews University Library and St Andrews Preservation Trust in providing material for use in this book.

Domesday extract used in timeline by kind permission of Alecto Historical Editions, www.domesdaybook.org
Aerial photographs reproduced under licence from Simmons Aerofilms Limited.
Historical Ordnance Survey maps reproduced under licence from Homecheck.co.uk

Every attempt has been made to contact copyright holders of illustrative material. We will be happy to give full acknowledgement in future editions for any items not credited. Any information should be directed to The Francis Frith Collection.

The colour-tinting in this book is for illustrative purposes only, and is not intended to be historically accurate

AS WITH ANY HISTORICAL DATABASE, THE FRANCIS FRITH ARCHIVE IS CONSTANTLY BEING CORRECTED AND IMPROVED, AND THE PUBLISHERS WOULD WELCOME INFORMATION ON OMISSIONS OR INACCURACIES

Contents

ST ANDREWS FROM THE AIR 1932 AF40387

Historical Timeline for St Andrews

Ancient Britain

c1500 BC First evidence of farming in the St Andrews area

Roman Britain

cAD100 Roman forts established in the area

c300 Roman influence in decline

AD80 Agricola's invasion

208 Severus invades Caledonia

368 Theodosius defeats the Picts of Valentia

Dark Ages

c565 Christianity arrives in Scotland when St Columbus lands on Iona

c877 Constantine II builds a church for the Culdees

c900 Culdees (companions of God) form a community at Kilrymont

563 Columba lands at Iona

761 Angus McFergus King of Dalriada and Strathclyde

841 Kenneth MacAlpin King of Scots

Late Medieval

1410 Teaching begins at the university

1527 Martyr Patrick Hamilton burned at the stake

1559 The Reformation. John Knox preaches at Holy Trinity Church and the cathedral is ransacked

1589 Town fortifications strengthened with the building of West Port gateway

1437-60 James II

1460-88 James III

1488-1513 James IV

1513-42 James V

1542-67 Mary Queen of Scots

1567-1603 James VI

Stuart Britain

1620 St Andrews given Royal Burgh status by James VI

(becomes)

1603-25 James I of England

1638 National Covenant

1642-49 Civil War

Georgian Era

1797 Town Council faces bankruptcy and sells the links to rabbit farmers

1821 James Cheape of Strathtyrum buys the links and returns them for the use of golfers

1832 Madras College founded

1790 Forth and Clyde Canal opened

1804 Invention of the power loom

1815 Battle of Waterloo

1833 Burgh Reform Act

1837-1901 Queen Victoria

Victorian Britain

1834 Royal and Ancient Golf Club formed. Its title was conferred by William III of Scotland

1852 First steam train arrives on new St Andrews Railway

1876 University faces closure with only 130 students

1897 Royal and Ancient recognised as the governing body for the rules of golf

1840 Rise of Chartism

1854-6 Crimean War

1876 Telephone invented

1887 Queen Victoria's Golden Jubilee

1899-1902 Boer War

1066 Norman invasion of England

1124 Augustinian priory founded by Bishop Robert

1153 St Andrews is elevated to burgh status by Bishop Robert with the support of David I

c1160 Cathedral foundations laid

c1200 Bishop Roger de Beaumont starts building St Andrews Castle

Middle Ages

1124-53 David I

1165-1214 William the Lion

1214-49 Alexander II

1263 Battle of Largs

1296 Battle of Stirling Bridge

1318 Cathedral consecrated

1332 English take St Andrews Castle, sparking a series of battles which see the castle changing hands many times

Late Medieval

1314 Battle of Bannockburn

1424-37 James I

1672 University students start wearing red gowns

Stuart Britain

1652-60 Commonwealth

1660 Restoration of the monarchy

1679-89 Covenanting Wars

1688-89 Glorious Revolution

1694-1701 Darien Scheme

1707 Act of Union

1754 Society of St Andrews Golfers formed

Georgian Era

1715 First Jacobite Rebellion

1745-6 Second Jacobite Rebellion

1775-83 American War of Independence

1904 Excavations of David Hay Fleming reveal remains of 14th-century priors

1911 First motorised fishing vessel uses the harbour

1913 First cinema opens, and green fees are imposed on visiting golfers

Edwardian Era

1901-10 Edward VII

1910-36 George V

1919 First civil air display over the sands

1930 New Picture House cinema opens in North Street

1933 Byre Theatre opens in Abbey Street in a cowshed on the site of a former dairy

1981 Award-winning film 'Chariots of Fire' filmed on West Sands

2001 Brand new Byre Theatre opens

20th Century Britain

1914-18 First World War

1919 First trans-Atlantic flight

1936-52 George VI

1939-45 Second World War

1975 Regions replace counties

1999 Scottish Parliament restored

CHAPTER ONE

A Town Built on Old Bones

THE PEOPLE OF ST ANDREWS in the Kingdom of Fife are proud and fiercely protective of their ancient town, and rightly so. The spires and towers, the rugged stone walls and ruins, the blue of the encircling sea, and in winter perhaps a dusting of snow on the distant hills to the north make a dramatic impression of a land and townscape little changed over the centuries. In the heart of this treasured town the impact of late 20th- and early 21st-century lifestyle changes are more apparent.

CAFÉ JANNETTA, SOUTH STREET 2005 ZZZ03925 (Shelagh Young)

Coffee houses existed in 18th-century St Andrews; Italian immigrants, including the Jannetta family, revived the café scene in the early 20th century with innovative products such as delicious ice creams and the exotic-sounding espresso and cappuccino.

Upmarket delicatessens selling olive ciabattas and truffle oil, designer clothes shops and jewellery shops huddle alongside clothing chain stores and stylish-looking cafés. Even on a dreich winter's day they are busy. While other Fife towns have clearly struggled to recover from the loss of industries such as mining and textiles, St Andrews seems lively and prosperous.

ST ANDREWS FROM THE SOUTH 1878 SA000487 (Courtesy of University of St Andrews Library)

There is much about this first impression that is only skin deep. Take the shops, whose gleaming well-lit windows hide little of the really old St Andrews. Rare is the purpose-built retail unit in this town. Instead, shops are housed in Edwardian, Victorian, Georgian and older buildings. Some hunch uncomfortably inside their unsuitable premises, and others are crammed happily into the old medieval street pattern as if this was how it was meant to be. There is concern about the sustainability of business in St Andrews. Independent retailers are considered to be under threat from high business rates and the steady creep of the charity shops, café chains and retail chains, which are accused of keeping rents unfeasibly high.

But what brought the whoosh and hiss of the cappuccino machine and the time and money to enjoy a lively café culture to the tiny town of St Andrews, and what keeps it going? The ancient university, a significant presence smack in the middle of town, is only part of the story. At night in term-time some of the 6000 resident students bring the kind of life to the streets which many residents feel they could do without. However, with students and university staff accounting for up to a third of the town's population, far fewer businesses would survive without their trade. But these temporary guests are small beer in comparison with the huge numbers of people who visit St Andrews every year. Some are simply drawn to its beautiful coastal setting. St Andrews has long been a seaside holiday destination. A harbour, miles of sandy beach and dunes, and craggy cliffs and rock pools mean that St Andrews appeals to many tastes. For the more active there is yachting, sand yachting, surfing and kite surfing; for others, entering the annual sand castle competition on the West Sands or the Cockshaugh Park Donkey Derby might be the peak of their exertions.

It is undoubtedly golf that brings most visitors into the town. Golfers the world over admit to dreaming of a round played on the famous Old Course - it is considered to be one of the world's most important, challenging and enjoyable golfing destinations.

Many locals enjoy a love/hate relationship with golf. Historians have called St Andrews a place of ruins. Now some St Andrews residents are saying that golf will ruin the place. They are proud and protective of their ancient streets and ruined castle, its jagged remains teetering high on a ragged, exposed cliff top to the northeast of the town. The ransacked cathedral and the ancient St Rule's Tower are reminders of four centuries of religious and political turmoil. Today's major battles are fought over development. While some seek to wrap the town in the preserving embrace of an all-encompassing Green Belt, others argue that more housing is vital. They fear that the town will suffocate under the twin pressures of inflated house prices and a fast growing hospitality industry which siphons profits off elsewhere while providing only low paid service-industry jobs to local people.

If the future of St Andrews is hotly debated, so is its past. What we know for sure is that the earliest signs of human habitation date from around 8000 BC. Excavations at

ST RULE'S TOWER 2005 ZZZ03926 (Shelagh Young)

ARMIT'S ST REGULUS SHORTBREAD ADVERTISEMENT c1935
ZZZ03936 (Courtesy of Norman Black)

St Rule's or St Regulus Tower is one of many local tourist attractions featured in advertisements such as this one from the 1930s. In the 1950s Armit's Bakery was taken over by Fisher & Donaldson, which still trades in Church Street.

Tentsmuir Forest across the River Eden to the north of St Andrews revealed Mesolithic flint tools and burnt hearths, evidence of a small, nomadic hunter-gatherer population which is thought to have lived on a diet that included wild cattle, deer, fish, shellfish, nuts and berries. It is assumed that they travelled into the area by sea and river using log boats, as the ground was even boggier then than it is now. Sea levels were higher, and many of today's inland areas would have been on the coast. Certainly, the presence of cod bones shows that sea fishing was part of Mesolithic life, although there are no known remains of boats to show us how they accomplished this feat.

By 1500 BC there is evidence of farming, with populations becoming more settled. The area was heavily wooded at this time and provided a rich hunting ground for boar, deer and other wild game. The development of Neolithic farming communities is backed by evidence from an important archaeological site at Balfarg, on the outskirts of Glenrothes to the south-east of St Andrews. Here shards of pottery, evidence of two large wooden structures, and a henge (a circular arrangement of ditches, banks and platform), together with other finds, suggest a ritual site.

Aerial photographs highlight the distinctive crop patterns that provide the evidence for ancient settlements close to St Andrews, and buried funerary urns and cists (burial mounds) discovered in the area provide clues to the lives of its earliest residents. Market Street yielded ancient cinerary urns during excavations in 1867, and burial cists have been found on a St Andrews headland. More recent excavations under St Andrews Public Library unearthed more than 50 bodies from a shallow grave, suggesting that the town is built on extensive medieval burial grounds.

Did you know?

At Balfarg in Fife archaeologists have found burnt traces of henbane, a natural hallucinogen, in a lump of porridge dating from the Neolithic era. The henbane plant is toxic to humans, but has traditionally been used in small quantities as a painkiller and sedative. Some also believed in its use as an aphrodisiac, although records do not show if it was swallowed or rubbed on the relevant body parts.

Roman forts were established in the area towards the end of the 1st century, but the Romans' power and influence in Scotland was in decline by the end of the 2nd century in the face of sustained opposition from the Picts. Some of what we know about the reputedly fierce and anti-Roman Picts comes from the Romans, but the later writings of the Venerable Bede tell us more. His 8th-century writing places St Andrews as the home territory of one of four southern Pictish groups and locates St Andrews in 'Fib', from which the contemporary county name of Fife is derived.

The development of Christianity, not surprisingly given the town's name, played a crucial role in the development of St Andrews. Christianity had come to Scotland in AD 565 with Ireland's St Columba landing on Iona. The Picts took up the rituals of the Celtic church of Columba, but by AD 850 Pictish St Andrews was no more. A group emerged who were inspired by the idea of the contemplative hermit-like life. These became known as the Culdees, meaning companions of God, and a small group (numbering thirteen by AD 927) gathered in St Andrews. Constantine II built a church on the inhospitable and exposed Lady Craig's Rock. It is thought that by the time the subsequent abbot, Constantine III, had died the church had moved higher on the headland to Kirkhill. Remains of this church dating from the 12th and 13th century were discovered in 1860, and the footings of Blessed Mary of the Rock make up one of the earliest St Andrews ruins that can still be seen today.

The Culdees were a powerful influence in early medieval St Andrews, but as the politics of church and state evolved they gradually lost power. In 1273 they were prevented from taking part in the election of a bishop. They survived excommunication, however, and still held significant amounts of land in the 14th century. However, their church was pulled down in 1559 by the Earl of Argyll, the Prior of St Andrews, following the Reformation.

STONE COFFINS, ST ANDREWS CATHEDRAL 1904 SA000431 (Courtesy of University of St Andrews Library)

These coffins were found in 1904 during excavations in the cathedral grounds by David Hay Fleming. They are thought to contain the bones of 14th-century Augustinian priors.

St Andrews

St Andrews was originally known as Cennrigmonaid. The link with St Andrew, a fisherman from Galilee and one of Christ's disciples, is a mystery. According to 13th-century legend, an angel commanded Bishop Rule to extract a tooth, a kneecap, an upper arm bone, and three fingers of the martyred St Andrew's right hand and to preserve them for future use in the 'utmost part of the world'. An 18-month journey followed, with the body parts taken from Greece to Kilrymont (St Andrews), where a cross was erected to defy the demons of the place and seven churches were built. An earlier legend written in the 12th century includes an angel guiding St Rule to the area, while a blinding flash of light and the voice of St Andrew commanded King Angus I to battle. Victory caused Angus to dedicate Cennrigmonaid to the greater glory of God and St Andrew, thus providing the perfect site for the holy relics.

The significance of St Andrews to Christians grew deeper: several legends tell of the coming to the town of parts of the body of St Andrew, relics of the crucified saint. However, there is no historical evidence of their arrival.

Traces of the stories surrounding the birth of St Andrews are seen in the place today. St Rule's Cave, just along from the castle ruins, is considered to have been talked up in the 18th century as an ancient holy place rather than being an actual place of any real historical significance. The impressive 108ft St Rule's (also known as St Regulus) Tower survives from the mid 11th century, and was the first church of the Augustinian priory of St Andrews. However, it was never referred to by this name until around 1500. This gives credibility to the idea that St Rule was invented by the monks to give St Andrews a spurious history which assured itself a prominent place on the ancient Christian map. This early case of spin doctoring certainly yielded good results. In 906 St Andrews became the seat of the Bishop of Alba (Gaelic for Scotland), and by 975 the diocese of St Andrews was greatly expanded to include land as far south as the Tweed.

THE CATHEDRAL RUINS, THE EAST GABLE AND ST RULE'S c1900
SA000359 (Courtesy of University of St Andrews Library)

Did you know?

St Andrew was martyred on a cross in Patras, Greece. Known as a crux decussata, the cross was formed of diagonal struts, unlike the perpendicular structure familiar from Christ's crucifixion. This pattern is seen today in the white diagonal cross, the saltire, of Scotland's national flag, and this cross of St Andrew is incorporated in the Union Jack.

The first significant church building in the town was probably built as a reliquary, the resting place for the alleged body parts of St Andrew and a focus for pilgrims wishing to worship near the holy relics. The historian Raymond Lamont-Brown dates the first church of St Rule to the 1070s, and describes it as a small chapel measuring 26ft by 20ft. It is the famous tower that was so impressive. Rising up 108ft, it became a major feature in the rolling landscape, guiding pilgrims across land and sea to their destination.

St Rule's Church was extended in the 12th century, and the tower still stands at 35m (115ft) amidst the ruins of both an early Augustinian priory and the great St Andrews Cathedral, which was the largest building ever constructed in medieval Scotland. Building work on the cathedral spanned the 12th to the 16th centuries, with stone quarried locally at Kinkell and Strathkinness. It is thought that the tiles which can still be seen in the ruined cathedral's nave were fired in workshops on the priory site. Certainly artisans worked at a number of trades within workshops on the site in medieval times.

The cathedral was consecrated by Bishop William Lamberton on 5 July 1318. In its grandest era, thought to be between 1440 and its destruction during the Reformation in 1599, the cathedral would not have been the quiet, echoing space we associate with ancient cathedrals today. Standing by its ruined walls with seagulls wheeling overhead, it is hard to imagine this vast space ever being described as busy or bustling. However, the cathedral was used both as the cathedral church of the diocese of St Andrews and as the church of the Augustinian order of canons regular who lived at the priory. It housed the famous relics, and was an important destination for pilgrims from all over Europe. Royalty and titled landowners made generous donations, including jewels for the reliquary. The place was filled with some of the best art and craft works of the period. Sumptuous wall hangings, fine stained glass, intricately carved wooden furnishings, exquisite chalices and ornately ornamented tombs brought richness to the grey stone structure.

The Chapel of Relics, tucked behind the high altar, was out of bounds to all but the most distinguished visitors. This did not stop less privileged pilgrims coming to pray. Any visitor to contemporary sites of pilgrimage, for example Lourdes, will understand that these places are attractive to those in pursuit

Did you know?

The original relics of St Andrew have never been found. It is possible that they were destroyed during the Reformation. Other alleged remains of St Andrew were kept in Amalfi in Italy, and in 1879 the Bishop of Amalfi presented Scottish Catholics with a piece of shoulder blade. Later, Pope Paul VI donated a further relic. These are now displayed at the national shrine to St Andrew in St Mary's Roman Catholic Cathedral in Edinburgh.

ST ANDREWS CATHEDRAL c1855
SA000404 (Courtesy of University of St Andrews Library)

of a miracle cure. Picture the scene in medieval St Andrews. The cathedral, visited by streams of the chronically ill and disabled, would have been a noisy and chaotic place. Lamont-Brown asks us to imagine 'the insane fettered in chains and cords to the pillars' and the 'sounds of the sick vomiting and the dying groaning'. No medieval settlement was free from the stench of poverty and inadequate sanitation, and the cathedral would have been no exception.

There are also fascinating accounts of strange offerings placed in the nave, including a worm vomited up by a pilgrim and a replica damaged leg and injured arm. Any number of homemade animal fat candles added their pungent smoke to the already fetid atmosphere.

THE VIEW FROM ST RULE'S c1900 SA000382 (Courtesy of University of St Andrews Library)

The first 13th-century west gable of the cathedral blew down in a storm almost as soon as it was completed. This surviving arch was built directly afterwards, and at that time the cathedral was over 320ft long. It was later extended to some 391ft in length.

All this came to an end following three days of vigorous preaching by John Knox at Holy Trinity Church in St Andrews on 14 June 1559. St Andreans were not only fired up by Knox and new ideas in religion, but they were also motivated by the mistrust caused by the growing political influence of France. A mob, supported behind the scenes by Protestant nobles including James Argyll, left the church and ransacked the cathedral, ending 400 years of worship there. The building was not demolished in one furious day, but gradually looted of its riches, including the actual fabric of the building. Many subsequent developments in St Andrews, including the harbour pier when it was repaired in the mid 1600s, have been created in part from stones taken from the once glorious cathedral.

The castle went the same way: the stones were used to repair the harbour in 1654 on the orders of the Town Council, and other parts were sold in 1656 to help fund repairs to the Long Pier. Bishop Roger de Beaumont had built the first castle on this site around 1100. The first known harbour was also established at this time at the mouth of the Kinness Burn, which still runs into the current harbour. The castle was sited round the headland to the north. By 1303 it was the royal residence of Edward I, having fallen into English hands several times in the 13th century. The castle was taken again by the English in 1332 and rebuilt in 1336, only to be destroyed when retaken by the Scots in 1337. Later it again became a fortified base for the bishops when Bishop Walter Trail of Blebo oversaw its reconstruction starting in 1385.

We can still see parts of the medieval castle, which had a slipway down to the sea at the foot of one of two towers, a Great Hall built into the east walls, and a partial moat. The sinister-looking 24ft-deep bottle dungeon survives. Its name reflects its design – it has a narrow neck which widens at the bottom - and it is dug from solid sandstone. John Knox claimed that many people had been imprisoned there, but opinion today is divided; some say that it was a food store rather than a prison. Whatever the purpose of the bottle dungeon, the castle certainly has a grisly history. The Protestant preacher George Wishart was strangled and burned in front of the castle on 1 March 1546 on the orders of Cardinal David Beaton. Revenge was swift, and in May of 1546 a small group gained entry to the castle and hacked Beaton to death. His body was hung on the east wall for the townspeople to see, then pickled in salt, sealed in a cist (an early form of coffin) and placed in the bottle dungeon before being taken for secret burial at Blackfriars in South Street.

IN ST ANDREW'S CASTLE 1887
SA000505 (Courtesy of University of St Andrews Library)

ST ANDREWS CASTLE AND THE BEACH c1900 SA000360 (Courtesy of University of St Andrews Library)

ST ANDREWS CASTLE AND THE BEACH WITH DANGER SIGN 2005 ZZZ03913 (Shelagh Young)

THE MEMORIAL TO PATRICK HAMILTON, NORTH STREET 2005 ZZZ03906 (Shelagh Young)

Wishart was not the first local martyr. Paul Craw was put to death in 1433, Patrick Hamilton was burnt at the stake for heresy in 1527, Henry Forrest followed in 1553, and so did Walter Myln in 1558. The Martyrs Monument, erected in 1842 and overlooking the Royal and Ancient Golf Club, commemorates these unfortunate men. The initials PH are also set in the pavement near St Salvator's Tower on North Street marking the spot at which Patrick Hamilton was burned.

At the ruined castle today it is possible to access an extraordinary pair of tunnels known as the mine and the countermine, which were rediscovered in 1879. They resulted from attempts by the 2nd Earl of Arran to retake the castle from the Protestants by burrowing into the foundations. The occupying forces retaliated by digging an intersecting tunnel. They achieved this amazing underground navigational feat using sound alone. Eventually the siege resulted in a victory for Arran, leaving the castle seriously damaged by cannon fire. It was again rebuilt before falling back into the hands of the Protestants in 1559 and going on to become the property of the Crown in 1587. Following all this turbulent history, the remains of the once Great Hall succumbed not to battle but to the forces of nature. It crashed into the sea in 1801, a victim of coastal erosion.

Defence against the sea has long been seen as more important to St Andreans than protection from human forces. The hills and bogs of Fife meant that for hundreds of years it was easier to travel to St Andrews by sea than by land; a safe harbour was crucial to maintaining the flow of pilgrims, and therefore wealth, into the town. Fishing became important to the local economy, and with strong currents, dangerous rocks and frequent storms, the area around St Andrews Bay was no place to linger without a nearby safe haven. In any case, it was not usual for Scottish towns to be heavily fortified; although remnants of an impressive set of protective city gates, known as ports, survive in St Andrews today, there was never an attempt to encircle the city with an impenetrable barrier.

The West Port at the western end of South Street still stands; it dates from 1589. It was remodelled to include side arches in 1843, and is the sole surviving fortified gateway in Scotland.

THE WEST PORT c1920 SA000378 (Courtesy of University of St Andrews Library)

THE PENDS SA000500 (Courtesy of University of St Andrews Library)

The Pends formed part of a vaulted gatehouse to the medieval priory; it dates from about 1350. The cathedral ruins to the left (unseen in this photograph) are still partly surrounded by the longest remaining expanse of medieval walling in Scotland.

Inside the ports the town's three main streets run westwards from the cathedral, and they are joined by an intersecting ladder of narrower lanes which still closely resembles the street plan shown in an early map from 1530. The majority of houses in medieval times were wooden. None of these survive.

The destruction wrought by the Reformation quite literally provided the foundations of much of the town we can see today. The ruined cathedral was used as a source of affordable building materials right up until the 18th century. Yet at the same time the events of the Reformation almost brought ruin to St Andrews. Its wealth and influence were founded on its importance as a religious site, and when this was stripped away the town shivered in the gloomy economic reality of its undeniably out-of-the-way location.

Up to this point St Andrews had experienced tremendous growth and affluence. In its prosperous early years the commercial life of St Andrews was dominated by the Trade Guilds, representing seven key trades of baker, flesher, shoemaker, smith, tailor, weaver and wright. In 1573, buoyed up by the trade brought by pilgrims, the busy town supported 72 bakers and 50 brewers. In medieval St Andrews there were five great annual fairs which attracted traders from quite a distance. Today, only the annual Lammas Fair on the second Monday and Tuesday of August survives, but as a modern funfair rather than the significant trading opportunity of old.

Mary Queen of Scots was a frequent visitor, and Queen Mary's House on the southern side of South Street, where she is said to have stayed in 1562, survives as a library for St Leonard's School. This house was built using the earliest known example of imported timber in Scotland. The dependence of medieval society on wood as building material and fuel is thought to have contributed to a shortage of timber in Scotland. Timbers from Queen Mary's House are known to have been felled at the turn of the 14th century, and may have come from Poland. They have certainly been traced to the eastern Baltic.

On several of her visits the queen enjoyed a game of golf. Golf had been played on the links (a natural turf and sand area on the coast which evolved in ancient times as the sea retreated) since the 14th century, and the game is thought to date back to around 1350.

Did you know?

Which is heavier, a pound of bread or a pound of cheese? In medieval St Andrews this was not a trick question. Scottish merchants used a variety of weights. English pounds, equivalent to 16 ounces, were used to weigh flour, bread and pot barley, while Dutch pounds (17 ounces) were used for meat. Tron pounds (22 ounces) were used for wool, butter, flax, cheese and hay. The boll (8 stone), firlot (2 stone), peck (8lbs) and lippie (92lbs) were old Scots measures also in use at the time.

It became so popular that in 1457 James II, who had become concerned that golf was distracting young men from their archery practice and reducing church attendance, banned the sport. Presumably this was not a particularly effective deterrent, because the ban was renewed by James III in 1471 and James IV in 1491.

Fortunately for modern golfers, James IV somehow became a convert to the game, and from 1502 the sport was revived under royal patronage.

QUEEN MARY'S HOUSE, SOUTH STREET c1900 SA000381
(Courtesy of University of St Andrews Library)

Did you know?

Sandwiched between Golf Place and Step Rock is a small grassy dip known as the Bow Butts. Archery was regularly practiced here right up to 1751. Winners of an annual competition received a medal, which they were allowed to fix to a silver arrow. The Bow Butts is now dominated by a bandstand, a seafood restaurant, and the entrance to the Sea Life Centre, making it rather unsuited to its original use.

THE BANDSTAND ON THE BOW BUTTS 2005
ZZZ03917 (Shelagh Young)

Nearly half a century on, the twin economic engines powering the town appear to be golf and the university. Both have their origins in medieval times, but it is the university's role in the life of the place which was of most significance in the years immediately following the Reformation. St Andrews became a seat of learning at the time of the Culdees. The control of training novices eventually passed to the Augustinians. The educational role of the institution was boosted when on 11 May 1410 Bishop Henry Wardlaw gained the support of King James I and others in founding a 'Studium Generale Universitatis', an institution with a mission to promote learning and support for the Catholic faith. At this stage the university still could not confer degrees, as university status could then only be granted by the Pope or the Holy Roman Emperor. In February 1414 Papal Bulls issued by the Antipope Benedict XIII, the only pope recognised by the Scottish aristocracy, arrived in St Andrews. These empowered the university to examine students (who in medieval times started their university education at 13), and to declare them qualified to teach others.

It is thought that the bacchanalian St Andrews tradition of Raisin Monday dates from the earliest days of the university. On Raisin Monday, first year students, known as bejants (male), and bejantines (female), parade in fancy dress. They reward their older student mentors with a bottle of wine, in place of the traditional raisins, and receive a 'ribald receipt in Latin'. Receipts in recent years have been written on such diverse items as a car and a baby's nappy.

By 1419 St Andrews University had acquired property in South Street which became known as the Chapel and College of St John the Evangelist. The university expanded to a site just west of this college in 1430, and in 1537 St Mary's College was founded there. Eventually there were three colleges: St Salvator's founded in 1450, St Leonard's in 1512, and St Mary's in 1537. Some parts of the earliest buildings remain. St Salvator's, founded by Bishop James Kennedy, can be seen in part today in North Street. The frontage is medieval; the tower dates from the 1450s, although its spire is a 16th-century replacement for the timber and lead spire destroyed in the castle siege of 1546. An additional parapet was built in 1846.

The 17th-century St John's House, which houses the university's history department, stands at 69 South Street. Oak timbers from trees felled in the late 13th century have been found inside St John's House. These hidden antiques form part of the fabric of the building, supporting reports that renovation, repair and new building in St Andrews often involved the cannibalisation of other building's parts.

St Leonard's College could now be called a 'virtual college', since it has no buildings of its own. Following a period of decline in the university's fortunes, it was re-established in 1972 for postgraduate study. The ancient college buildings now form part of the independent St Leonard's School; visitors can gain entrance to the chapel, formerly a resting place for pilgrims.

St Mary's is based in South Street for the

ST MARY'S COLLEGE BY JOHN OLIPHANT c1767 SA000513 (Courtesy of University of St Andrews Library)

ST SALVATOR'S COLLEGE BY JOHN OLIPHANT c1767 SA000514 (Courtesy of University of St Andrews Library)

Bishop Kennedy and his Mint

Bishop Kennedy (c1408-65) was an influential figure in Scottish politics. He was close to both King James II and King James III, and his role as trusted advisor led to his being granted a rare privilege. On 14 June 1452 Kennedy was granted a charter allowing him to mint coins. The copper pennies and farthings produced by Kennedy's mint are very sought after by collectors. Although they were used widely throughout the east of Scotland, very few examples survive today. It is assumed that the coins were minted in St Andrews Castle. Coins had been minted in St Andrews before on the authority of Alexander III (1241-86) and later John Baliol (1250-1313). But Kennedy's coins are thought to have been unique in medieval Britain, for they were minted under his authority and bore the archbishop's own coat of arms.

study of divinity, and still houses the School of Divinity, partly in 16th-century buildings. Several ancient buildings can be seen where they bound the quad. The Principal's house was built in 1544 as was Frater Hall, and the Stair Tower followed in 1552. Both the quads at St Mary's and St Salvator's are open to visitors.

Drawing some of its strength from a Scottish desire for independence and an aversion to allowing Oxford and Cambridge to dominate the academic life of Britain, the university survived the battles over faith and many subsequent political struggles. It did not emerge unscathed; but having educated the ruling elite in Scotland for so many years, there is no doubt that the university has always enjoyed support in high places. However, it suffered from the shift in power to Edinburgh and Glasgow universities following the Act of Union in 1707. It is true to say that the decline of St Andrews as a whole began substantially earlier, when the Reformation triggered what has been described as a 300-year depression.

Nevertheless, by the 18th century both town and gown were in desperate need of revival.

CHAPTER TWO

The Return of the Gentlefolk

ST ANDREWS BECAME a Royal Burgh under James VI in 1620. This suggests that its fortunes were continuing to rise. Nothing could be further from the truth. St Andrews had been a Royal Burgh in all but title for some time.

It is possible that the formal granting of Royal Burgh status was in recognition of improvements to the running of the town following a period of lawlessness and corruption. By 1697, when the town was hit by a proposal to move the university to Perth, the place had been in decline for the best part of a century. There was fishing, though not on the scale of the more successful nearby Fife harbours such as Anstruther and Pittenweem to the south, and there was little to recommend life in St Andrews.

Contemporary accounts paint a grim picture. Closing the Forth crossing and other routes into the town failed to prevent serious outbreaks of plague in 1585 and again in 1605. The population quickly fell to less than 4,000 people. If it was not the plague or some other disease that killed people, it was starvation. Measures to introduce local taxation to help support the sick and the poor were reputedly thwarted owing to widespread corruption.

Continuing problems with silting and damage to the protective harbour walls hindered access to St Andrews. Trade dwindled, and desperate attempts were made to secure funds to repair the harbour. A series of begging missions to Dunfermline, Edinburgh and other wealthy neighbours secured a temporary reprieve for the town's councillors. The harbour was repaired, but the town was no longer the prosperous place it had been. The historian Raymond Lamont-Brown quotes a contemporary description of late 17th-century St Andrews:

'This place being now only a village, where most part farmers dwell, the whole streets filled with dunghills, which are exceedingly noisome and ready to infect the air, especially at this season Autumn, when the herring guts are exposed in them ...'

Fife as a whole was struggling in the early 18th century. The impact of the Civil War had been devastating in the Highlands, but the effects did not stop there. In his mission to defeat the Royalists and the Covenanters in Scotland, Cromwell's General Monck commanded forces which all but destroyed many of the settlements right along the east coast of Scotland. For example, 500 civilians were slaughtered in Dundee, and Kirkcaldy was virtually laid to waste. Trade and manufacturing were concentrated in the south and west of the region, which enjoyed better harbour facilities and easier access to other significant settlements such as Edinburgh. But even they were not immune from depression. The 1707 Act of Union seemed to hasten the decline of the ports. In 1723 Daniel Defoe wrote of Burntisland: 'What is the best harbour in the world without ships?'

St Andrews was badly affected by this general decline. The merchants of St Andrews saw demand for fish and wool dwindle. At the same time, inshore fishing was hit by shifts in the levels of available fish stocks. Further damage to the harbour and the local fish drying grounds as a result of storms, then a series of crop failures, exacerbated the town's problems. After a devastating maritime disaster in 1765 in which a dozen local fishermen died in a storm, it took until 1803 for local fishing to revive. A sawmill and a distillery at the port of Guardbridge in the Eden estuary to the west of St Andrews managed to weather the lean years. However, in terms of trade, St Andrews never recovered its pre-Reformation buzz. Medieval accounts tell of 200 to 300 ships moored in the area at the time of the great annual Senzie fair, with traders from many countries queuing up to sell spices, fine cloth, jewels and other luxury items. A modest trade in timber and agricultural products never matched those glory years.

THE ROCK AND SPINDLE c1850
SA000417 (Courtesy of University of St Andrews Library)

A WRECK ON THE WEST SANDS c1890
SA000432 (Courtesy of University of St Andrews Library)

Even in a calm sea the rocky St Andrews coastline could be treacherous. The identity of the large wrecked ship is not known, although it is thought to be either the Norwegian 'Elizabeth', wrecked in March 1891, or the 'Wilhelm', a schooner from Riga wrecked in October 1898.

Despite these problems, St Andrews always sustained a small population of fisherfolk. Their homes, clustered around the east end of North Street, were redeveloped many years ago. The All Saints Episcopal church rectory was built in this area in 1938, and in 1971 the university's Gannochy House was built in place of the slums. Gannochy House is currently a student's residence.

Did you know?

In 1792 St Andrews had a population of only 2,500 residents, but an astonishing 42 taverns are recorded. Fishing was a significant industry at the time, and although the local fleet was small, it is possible that visiting crews were an important source of business.

In the late 17th century the university's professors used the increasing dereliction of the town as a basis for their unsuccessful bid to move the university to Perth. They commented on plaster falling from the walls of houses, and also protested that things had become so bad that they had to travel to Edinburgh to buy their 'hattes'. If not all their arguments carried the weight and rigour one might expect from intelligent men, St Andrews was indisputably in trouble. As fortunes fell, so did income from taxation; in 1797 the Town Council, facing bankruptcy, sold the famous Links, which were turned into a rabbit farm.

Did you know?

In the 17th century elders of the church helped police morals and behaviour by making regular visits to the homes of St Andreans. 'Boyes' and their poor behaviour was a regular item of concern. Absence from church on the Sabbath due to playing 'at the gouf' seemed to afflict all ages, and records show that elders were sent to ascertain the identities of these sinful characters so that further action could be taken.

In 1806 the town was described in Robert Forsyth's 'The Beauties of Scotland' as having buildings of a size and grandeur 'evidently disproportioned to any business or active employment' carried out in the place - these were 'falling into ruin from the want of present wealth or energy.' Even many of the wealthier merchant families in St Andrews had fallen on hard times. It is hard to imagine the solid-looking buildings which are so much admired today falling into disrepair, but many were.

The absence of many sizeable Georgian buildings and the presence of so much grand Victorian architecture tell us much about the chronology of the renaissance in St Andrews. However, there were some families who weathered the chilly financial climate of the post-Reformation town who were able to build relatively modest homes in the Georgian period. Some of these beautiful houses can be seen today, and still more have a stylish Georgian façade tacked on to a much older building lying behind. A good example of a 16th/17th-century building with Georgian additions can be seen at 1 South Street near the Pends. The Roundel is now restored as a postgraduate study centre for St Mary's College.

Other typical examples of development in the Georgian period include Castlemount on the Scores. This surviving Georgian home has traded as a small hotel offering splendid views out to the castle ruins. Another was the Ardgowan Hotel at 2 Playfair Terrace, which was created from two Georgian terraced buildings designed by the architect Sir William Playfair.

THE ROUNDEL, SOUTH STREET 2005 ZZZ03920 (Shelagh Young)

"ARDGOWAN"

Board Residence

PLAYFAIR TERRACE

Two minutes from 1st Tee Old Course, and Shore. Near Station. Every Comfort. Good Food. Lovely enclosed Garden.

TERMS MODERATE. *Telephone* **263.**

Proprietresses: MRS. & THE MISSES BENNIE.

AN ADVERTISEMENT FOR ARDGOWAN HOTEL c1930 ZZZ03948 (Courtesy of Norman Black)

The upturn in St Andrews' fortunes was apparent by the mid 19th century. The 1801 census records 4203 inhabitants. In 1851 this had grown to 6740, still a smaller population than the town had known pre-Reformation. By this time changes across Scotland had begun to have an impact on the people of Fife. A burgeoning urban-based middle class were looking to the seaside and to rural areas for a relaxing escape from the increasingly industrialised, dirty and overcrowded towns. Also, Fife was rich in coal, and had developed an effective textiles industry focused on linen. Cloth was in demand at home and eventually for export to the growing empire. Local farmers could supply meat and dairy products to growing city populations.

Changes outside the town presented new opportunities for trade. Gradually the harbour came back to life. Alongside the newly

The Textile Industry

The textile trade seems to have been one of the few local industries to have weathered the hard times in the 17th and 18th centuries. Spinning and weaving was a cottage industry, with 52 working looms recorded in the mid 18th century. Dying was done outdoors on a larger scale. Working on the slopes leading down to Kinness Burn at the east end of the South Haugh, the dyers stoked fires beneath great vats. The yarn or fabric was stirred with huge paddles and beaten with mallets to ensure even distribution of colour. The heavy wet material was winched out to be cleansed in running water. The stench of the boiling dyes was unpopular, and so the dyers carried out their trade at a reasonable distance from the main residential streets. Subject to the exacting quality standards set by the Guilds, at one time only master dyers were allowed to use substantive dyes such as seaweed, acorns and grass. Others of lesser experience were allowed only to work with fugitive dyes such as elder, bracken and daffodil which, despite the use of fixing techniques, would more readily fade.

established herring fleet, boosted by government funding, were vessels loading coal, iron and agricultural produce such as oats and potatoes. These were destined for use in the fast-growing urban areas. The first regular stagecoach started running to and from Cupar in 1829, but before the arrival of the railway in nearby Leuchars in 1847 the sea still afforded the easiest route into St Andrews. The roads in Fife at this time remained very poor. A system of tolls started to generate the income necessary to improve the highways, but travel was slow and mainly by expensive privately-hired carriage. Regular ferries started to sail to Dundee and in 1830 to Leith, making it possible for people to make relatively speedy and affordable visits to the town.

Did you know?

Herring is considered a delicacy in many European countries. A British Government bounty paid to fisherfolk selling herring abroad helped boost trade in the early 19th century. Government payments of £3 per ton were also made to owners of boats over 60 tons. These financial incentives, coupled with the arrival of the railways allowing speedier despatch of the fish, facilitated a 19th-century fishing boom in Scotland.

At the turn of the century St Andrews also began benefiting from an injection of the kind of reforming zeal which transformed many of Britain's disease-ridden cities. In 1781 the Town Council contracted a Perth-based plumber to install a clean drinking water supply. By 1793 St Andrews had a system of street wells fed by lead pipes supplying safe, clean drinking water to all its residents. The council was also behind the revival of fishing. Fishermen were persuaded to move down from the Shetlands by the promise that they would be paid ten shillings a week when it was not possible to go to sea.

It seems that these enterprising moves did not reap immediate rewards in terms of increased income for the town as a whole. As mentioned earlier, the Town Council suffered the ignominy of near bankruptcy, saved only by the sale of the golfing links to Thomas Erskine, who subsequently leased the land to farmers intent on raising rabbits. A legal battle ensued between the Society of St Andrews' Golfers (which had been formed in 1754 to oversee an annual golfing competition, and was to become the Royal and Ancient in 1834) and the farmer. This resulted in the courts upholding the rights of golfers to access the land, but did not prevent the Links being damaged by the burrowing beasts. We may be thankful that the local Laird of Strathtyrum, a keen golfer and member of the Society, bought the land in 1821 for the purpose of protecting it.

The upturn in St Andrews' fortunes continued at a slow pace. Weaving employed many people in their own homes until mechanisation overcame the handloom weavers. Those wealthy merchant families that survived the decline of the town often did so by switching to trading in alcohol and associated materials. Malting, the preparation of barley for use in distilling and brewing, survived the long recession, despite being hit by what the Scots perceived as a very unfair Malt Tax in 1724. There was a vigorous local trade in wines and spirits. These were legitimately imported, although mainly into larger ports such as Leith, but smuggling was also a feature of life in most small Scottish ports. St Andrews was no exception. Inns and alehouses existed, but a great deal of alcohol was sold and consumed in private houses. Drunkenness was a much-complained-about problem exhibited by both students and locals.

Did you know?

Binge drinking is not a problem unique to modern Britain. Drunkenness also was rife in St Andrews in the early 19th century. Violent fights in the street were common, as were attacks on students. A woman who sold spirits from her house was so concerned about the inebriated state of a student customer that she followed him home. Unfortunately both tumbled from the cliff above Witch Lake, and were killed.

One of the big changes which stimulated the 19th-century renaissance of St Andrews was the increasing inability of wealthier families to offer their children a ready-made livelihood as they entered adulthood. As traditional businesses failed to thrive and fortunes dwindled, the merchant classes seized upon new opportunities for social and economic advancement via entry into a profession. The sons who would have inherited successful import/export businesses in better times were now encouraged to achieve a high standard of education in order to make their living as doctors and lawyers, and to take advantage of the opportunities being offered by colonialism. The Buddo family was one which forged this new path. Originally weavers by trade, by the early 18th century they had recognised the need to change direction. David Buddo, born in 1800, made his fortune as a surgeon and retired to St Andrews following a career in the Indian Medical Service. It was Buddo who built the substantial Kinburn House in Kinburn Park, now a local history museum.

THE TOWN HALL c1850 SA000403
(Courtesy of University of St Andrews Library)

THE TOWN HALL 2005 ZZZ03924 (Shelagh Young)

Similarly Sir Hugh Lyon Playfair, then Major Playfair and son of the principal of the United College, retired to St Andrews in 1834 following a career with the East India Company. He was elected to the position of provost in 1842 and set about modernising St Andrews.

Playfair's legacy is seen in St Andrews' broad streets, renovated quay and a town comparatively well defended from the encroaching sea, but his actions remain controversial. Some

The original town hall or tollbooth was demolished in 1862, and its 19th-century replacement now houses a record shop as well as function and meetings rooms. The Community Council meets here monthly.

called his plans for the town 'handsome', and few fail to appreciate the importance of his measures designed to improve sea defences. However, others have referred to him as a bully and a vandal. Under his direction street lights went in, making St Andrews the best lit town of its day, pavements were laid, and streets widened. However, old buildings were flattened as side streets were created, and he is accused of destroying the old tollbooth in Market Street and replacing it with a 'pretentious' Town Hall.

Playfair died in 1861 before many of his ideas were realised and just as the social and economic renaissance of the place was taking off.

Did you know?

This house has survived the Playfair modernisation process with its external stairs intact. Even Sir Hugh Lyon Playfair's nephew admitted that his uncle may have overstepped the mark on some occasions. His drive to redesign St Andrews is reputed to have led to some rather drastic night-time architectural vandalism. Nephew Lord Playfair writes that 'ancient stairs which projected from the houses into the streets so as to block the thoroughfares were removed during the darkness of night and the occupants had to devise new modes of entrance.'

SOUTH CASTLE STREET 1972
SA000427 (Courtesy of University of St Andrews Library)

PLAYFAIR'S MEMORIAL IN THE CATHEDRAL GROUNDS 2005 ZZZ03918 (Shelagh Young)

Playfair's redevelopment plans were backed by a series of public health initiatives overseen by Dr John Adamson, who held the post of Medical Officer of Health. Many suggest that Adamson's work was far more influential in creating a turnaround in quality of life for St Andreans, and consequently in helping to fuel the growth of the town.

Adamson died in 1870, but he lived long enough to see the outcome of the beneficial changes for which he had lobbied. In the 1861 Parochial Directory for Fife and Kinross, St Andrews is described in glowing terms. This account gives us some clues as to the source of its renewed prosperity:

'St Andrews derives its modern importance mainly from the number and prosperity of its educational establishments, joined to the healthiness of its situation, and the facilities it affords for sea bathing purposes; and, on this account, the number of its gentry far exceeds that of other towns of a similar size. It is a practise with many of our country gentlemen, instead of boarding their children in a university town, to make the city their residence during the period that their children are receiving their education, the junior branches at the Madras College, and the senior at the University; and, as there are also several hundreds of young gentlemen boarded in the city, the result is such a circulation of capital as compensates for the want of trade and manufactures, public works, &c'.

Did you know?

John Adamson believed that many people were ignorant of the dangers of unsanitary conditions in Scottish towns. He is quoted as saying that 'they have no objections to the dunghills or dirt, or filthy privies, or foul ashpits, or rarely cleaned cow byres or pigstyes'. He argued that the death rates should be monitored, and a legal duty placed on local authorities to report on sanitary conditions whenever the rate exceeded an agreed maximum limit.

John Adamson

As well as being a champion of improved public health, the talented John Adamson (1809-1870) is known as the father of Scottish photography. While secretary of the Literary and Philosophical Society he used his knowledge of chemistry to improve the calotype process. This was the use of paper negatives to produce photographic prints which had been discovered by William Henry Fox Talbot and introduced to John by Sir David Brewster, principal of the St Andrews colleges. Brewster was an admirer of Talbot's and also, incidentally, the inventor of the kaleidoscope. In 1842 John worked with his brother Robert, and the advances they made were such that the following year Robert moved to Edinburgh to produce calotypes for a living with D O Hill. (Robert died aged 26 in 1847, leaving a wonderful body of work behind him). John Adamson continued to develop and adapt new photographic processes. He was commissioned to take portraits, and many of these survive, together with landscapes and street scenes. His style was unusually natural, with subjects looking comparatively relaxed for an era in which heavy cameras and slow exposures placed severe restrictions on the art of photography. He is credited with encouraging his one-time laboratory assistant Thomas Rodger to set up the first photographic studio in St Andrews in 1849 when he was only 17. His father, also Thomas Rodger, exhibited photographs in Edinburgh, but modestly described his son's work as being superior. Rodger junior trained the Hungarian Ivan Szabo, who went on to exhibit work at the Photographic Society of Scotland's exhibitions and to open a studio in Edinburgh. St Andrews University Library holds over 300,000 photographic images, many of them by Brewster, Adamson, Rodger and other pioneers of photography, and is one of the most important collections of historic photographs in Scotland.

THE ADAMSON HOME, 127 SOUTH STREET 1862
SA000502 (Courtesy of University of St Andrews Library)

COMPOSITE OF SCENES AND WORTHIES OF ST ANDREWS 1876 SA000498
(Courtesy of University of St Andrews Library)

This composite picture showing notable and worthy people of St Andrews is thought to have been used for promotional purposes at the studio of Thomas Rodger.

Madras College, which is now a comprehensive school, was the brainchild of an early and well-educated returnee to St Andrews. The Reverend Dr Andrew Bell was born in St Andrews in 1753. His father, described both as a barber and a wig maker, was a local magistrate, and appeared to be very ambitious for his son. Dr Bell studied at the university, and following a period working as a tutor in America, eventually became a clergyman and travelled to India as a chaplain to the regiments of the East India Company.

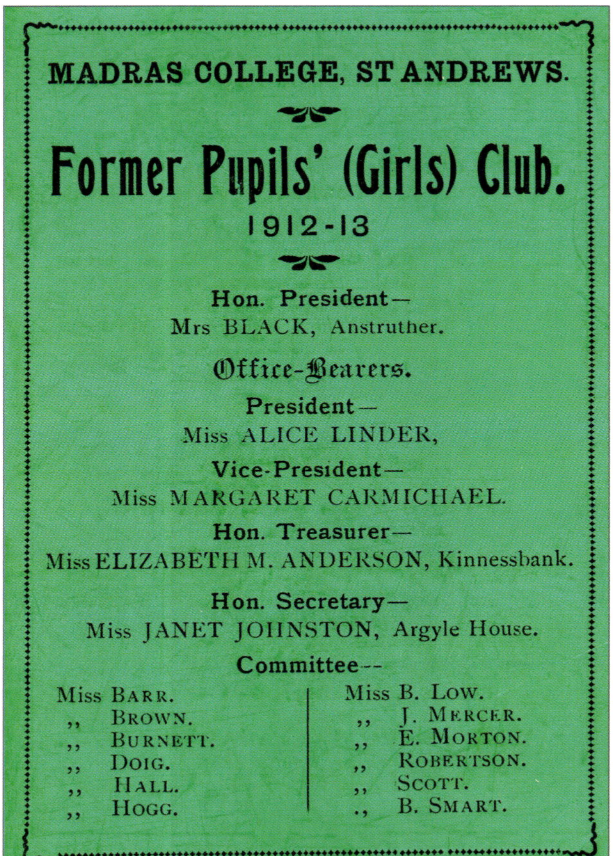

MADRAS COLLEGE, ST ANDREWS.

Former Pupils' (Girls) Club.

1912-13

Hon. President—
Mrs BLACK, Anstruther.

Office-Bearers.

President—
Miss ALICE LINDER,

Vice-President—
Miss MARGARET CARMICHAEL.

Hon. Treasurer—
Miss ELIZABETH M. ANDERSON, Kinnessbank.

Hon. Secretary—
Miss JANET JOHNSTON, Argyle House.

Committee--

Miss BARR.	Miss B. LOW.
,, BROWN.	,, J. MERCER.
,, BURNETT.	,, E. MORTON.
,, DOIG.	,, ROBERTSON.
,, HALL.	,, SCOTT.
,, HOGG.	., B. SMART.

MEMBERSHIP CARD FOR THE MADRAS FORMER PUPILS' (GIRLS) CLUB 1912-1913
ZZZ03943 (Courtesy of St Andrews Preservation Trust Museum)

Bell continued to work in education with the children of soldiers. Lack of staff led him to involve older children in helping younger children to learn, and this method seemed to get good results. Dr Bell travelled widely promoting what he called the 'Madras System', and he eventually returned to St Andrews to found a school. He died in 1832 before his ambitions was fully realised, although he had sold further land to fund a similar school in Cupar, which is now the local Bell Baxter comprehensive school. It is thought that over 10,000 schools worldwide had adopted all or part of the Madras system of education by the time of Bell's death.

In 1833 Madras College was opened in South Street. The building work had been funded by Bell, and the pupils came from a merger between the old grammar school (based between the site of the ancient Blackfriars Church and Lade Braes Lane) and the so-called 'English' school housed behind the Church of the Holy Trinity. The school also attracted pupils from outside the town. Co-educational from the start, the school reflected the social values of the day; very few girls attended in the early years, and there were no women teachers. Perhaps an investment of 15p a quarter for teaching fees was considered too much for daughters? Certainly the facilities left something to be desired. Lavatories were not introduced until

THE RUINS OF BLACKFRIARS MONASTERY AND MADRAS COLLEGE 1887 SA000504 (Courtesy of University of St Andrews Library)

1835, and the school was a chilly place. The masters were considered to be fairly eccentric even by 19th-century standards. It is reported that the classics master, Edward Woodford, kept a small pig at his home in part of the Madras building.

The façade of the original Madras College building stands behind a fragment of a 16th-century building which originally housed the Dominican black friars. Parts of this ancient property were still inhabited when building work began, and its further remains were demolished during the building of the college. A redeveloped and modernised school now shelters behind this impressive frontage.

The Jacobean style building became a symbol of the new St Andrews. When its foundation stone was laid in 1832, it was already known to be the largest public building to be developed in St Andrews since the Reformation. The school has been operating on two sites since 1967. Although the old building is not ideal for teachers and pupils by modern standards, this decision not to abandon the original building points to the symbolic importance of the school to the town.

The passing of the 1872 Education (Scotland) Act helped to improve further the provision of education in St Andrews through the creation of school boards to oversee standards. In 1890 the Education Act ensured that education became free for all, in so far as the cost was met through general local rates rather than fees per child - or even per class, as once had been the system at Madras College. This quashed the growth in small-scale private schooling which had mushroomed in St Andrews. At one point so-called 'adventure' schools, named for their financially adventurous nature rather than for their learning opportunities, were run by an assortment of people ranging from cobblers to clergymen. Some of these private initiatives met the practical needs of poorer people. For example, the Fisher School was set up with evening classes for working children of the fishing community. Daytime was spent baiting lines or mending nets, while basic literacy was taught at night. The Fisher School became known as the East Infants School, and although it had been set up by the fishing community, it was popular with a wide range of families.

FISHER WOMEN 1845 SA000401 (Courtesy of University of St Andrews Library)

Shabby housing in North Street was home to fishing families. Some children can be seen with the women here, and they were probably working on baiting lines. (This photograph by D O Hill and Robert Adamson comes from their 'Series of Calotype Views of St Andrews', published in Edinburgh in 1846).

BURGH SCHOOL CERTIFICATE 1911 ZZZ03944
(Courtesy of St Andrews Preservation Trust Museum)

The Burgh School was developed in Abbey Walk in 1889. It was the junior secondary school until 1963, when all secondary schools in Fife became comprehensive. Then the Burgh School and Madras College merged to form the present Madras College.

The provision of education for girls was a subject of great interest in the latter half of the century. Elizabeth Garret Anderson, born in 1836, became the first British woman to enter the medical profession; this was partly as a result of support from tutors at St Andrews University, who offered her an education in general medicine when other institutions turned her down. Other women pioneers wanted improved provision in education for women, and this fuelled the development of one of St Andrews' more successful independent schools, St Leonard's. A Ladies Education Association had been formed in St Andrews, and links were made between these forward-thinking women of St Andrews and proponents of the women-only Girton College at Cambridge, which was eventually founded in 1869.

An early Girton graduate, Louisa Lumsden, came to St Andrews on 2 October 1877 as headmistress of the new St Leonard's Girls' School in Queens Street. The school moved to its present site in Pends Road in 1882. By this time Louise had resigned. She remained a prominent local figure until her death aged 95 in 1935. A one-time warden of University Hall, Louisa Lumsden continues to feature as one of the characters of St Andrews during the annual Kate Kennedy day parades.

One of the less well-known stories about St Leonard's is that it was the birthplace of lacrosse in Scotland. The game is thought to have first been played there in 1890, and old girl Rosabelle Sinclair is thought to have established the first women's lacrosse team in the USA. In 2005 the Scottish national women's lacrosse team included several players educated at St Leonard's.

The importance of the influence of education on the fortunes of St Andrews continues today with the role of the university. However, for many years this institution also teetered on the brink of disaster. In 1876 the university authorities had more to worry about than their forebears had when they worried about shopping for 'hattes'. The student roll was down to 130, and the institution faced closure. An investigation by the Royal Commission which started in 1826 had already stimulated improvements to facilities and the running of the university, but student numbers continued to fall. In 1881 a merger with the University College of Dundee was proposed, and by 1898 a merged school of medicine had been established in Dundee.

St Andrews had been the first university to enrol women in 1862. Women were not able to actually graduate from the university until 1892, a year ahead of the founding in 1893 of St Hilda's College in Oxford for women students.

All these measures, combined with strong leadership into the 20th century, ensured slow but steady improvement in numbers and reputation. Today the university is a major economic force in the life of St Andrews, and it is hard to believe that such a thriving institution came within a whisker of closure just as life in St Andrews was beginning to look up.

Suffragettes in St Andrews

Some think that St Andrews University saved itself by admitting women and by being relatively early in achieving equality in terms of enabling women to graduate. This may have also been influenced by campaigning pressure. In November 1867 the first branch of the National Society for Women's Suffrage was constituted in Edinburgh, and by 1871 there was a branch in St Andrews. A leading figure in the local movement was Louisa Lumsden, headmistress of St Leonard's School from 1877 to 1882. In 1897 she became warden of the first residence for women at St Andrews University. She had been president of the Aberdeen Suffrage Society, and when a major suffrage rally took place in London in 1913 she was one of the speakers. She also organised suffrage summer schools at the university. Not all campaigners embraced violence, but in 1913 a threat to damage the golf links, believed to come from the suffrage movement, forced 330 local volunteers to mount round-the-clock protection. In June of that year the railway station at Leuchars was burned down in an arson attack, and part of the new Gatty Marine Laboratory was also destroyed by fire. Two messages left at the laboratory ('Take heed of the women's rebellion' and 'We need to be goaded, like oxen we are, into a trot') fuelled speculation about the role of suffragettes in the crime, as did the fact that the director of the laboratory had chaired an anti-suffrage meeting. The local suffrage society condemned the action, and it is still not known whether these acts of violence were the work of suffragettes.

CHAPTER THREE

The Growth of Learning and Leisure

MANY TOWNS IN SCOTLAND are still mourning the loss of jobs which were associated with the massive growth in manufacturing industry in the 19th and early 20th centuries. It seems odd, then, to attribute today's prosperity in St Andrews to the almost complete absence of any significant industrialisation. Yet this is how the story of St Andrews unfolds.

Picture the scene. Britain's increasingly industrialised towns such as Glasgow, Birmingham, Sheffield and London simmer in a miasma of sooty skies, toxic fumes from a wide range of dirty industries, and the stench of the slums. But St Andrews glimmers in its spectacular seaside setting. Here there is clean air, the salty tang of the sea, the wide open skies and mountain views on the horizon. The wide, quiet streets and cosy narrow wynds offer a peaceful escape from the grimy cities. Even if Sir Walter Scott had not bamboozled the public with his highly romanticised view of Scotland, St Andrews appeared on first impressions to offer much to visitors that was in short supply at home.

The wealthy upper middle classes were looking for sanctuary and restoration. They had time and money for leisure, and golf seemed to offer the perfect open-air pastime for gentlemen successful in business and with time on their hands. Salt water was seen as curative, and trips to the seaside were becoming increasingly fashionable. St Andrews started to rise to the challenge of satisfying a new kind of tourist - not pilgrims as such, but people equally devoted to finding some sort of revitalisation of body and soul.

In his role as provost, Playfair spotted the opportunity to attract more visitors to St Andrews and to create the infrastructure which would allow the town to develop. He teamed up with distiller Robert Haig to bring the railway to St Andrews. This would not only deliver visitors more quickly and easily than ever before, it would also bring in large quantities of building materials not available locally. Supplies of the locally quarried Strathkiness stone were available, but relatively expensive. Rapid development would need affordable bricks, slates, granite and timber, and the railway was the key to reducing transport costs and speeding up delivery.

Playfair and Haig were successful. In 1852, ten years after Playfair was first elected provost, the St Andrews Railway Company celebrated the opening of a new branch line with a fourteen-minute journey from Leuchars to St Andrews enjoyed by local dignitaries. This was followed by dinner at the Town Hall. The low development cost of £5,625 was originally a clear cause for celebration; but although the line opened to passengers immediately, problems soon emerged. By 1858 strengthening work was required. Shoddy workmanship was blamed for this, and for the fact that in everyday use the travel time to connecting trains at nearby Leuchars was an astonishingly lengthy 20 minutes.

At first the station was out of town. Known as the Links Station, and situated on the site of today's Old Course Hotel, it was more convenient for golfers than for the residents of St Andrews. Another station was built in 1887 when a new line linked St Andrews to more towns in the East Neuk of Fife. The new station was nestled in a cutting, now filled and transformed into a car park, at the west end of the town close to today's bus station. It had a broad, island platform under a large canopy with wrought ironwork details. You can still see a severed bridge which once carried the railway across the road which leads out of St Andrews to Guardbridge; this was the extension from the Links Station. It continued to be used for many years as a goods yard until the closure of the railway created the perfect vacant site for the hotel.

The advent of railway travel to St Andrews certainly delivered more visitors, and changes in the town made it a more attractive place to be. On 1 January 1855 Playfair announced that:

'In consequence of the cleanliness of the streets and the taste displayed in ornamenting the houses, the fame of St Andrews has spread abroad. This well-deserved celebrity is rapidly extending. Strangers from every quarter are induced to reside amongst us.'

NORTH STREET FROM THE WEST 1887
SA000507 (Courtesy of University of St Andrews Library)

MARKET STREET FROM THE WEST 1896

SA000486 (Courtesy of University of St Andrews Library)

Playfair's legacy can been seen in these broad, clean streets with many street lamps. The memorial fountain to the Victorian writer George John Whyte-Melville (1821-1878) which the three men appear to be inspecting stands on the site of the demolished tollbooth in Market Street. Today it is used as a planter.

Playfair died in 1861, but his ambitions for St Andrews continue to be realised. His comments about 'strangers from every quarter' certainly hold true today. When the Forth rail bridge opened in 1890, access to St Andrews from Edinburgh and the south was made even easier, putting the town on track for a long-lasting tourism boom. Unfortunately, not everyone was pleased with Playfair's achievements, and even before his death there were rumblings of protest. Worries about the built environment are echoed in today's concerns to protect what is beautiful and unique about St Andrews. Other negative comments were more about preserving a certain way of life, or, as some expressed it at the time, maintaining 'certain standards'. The problem, as some saw it, was that St Andrews had begun to attract the wrong kind of people. Despite the efforts of the Royal and Ancient Club (formed in 1834 under the patronage of William IV) to attract a superior class of member, visitors to St Andrews were often criticised by the locals. Complaints of drunkenness amongst the tourists were common.

Gradually the potential of St Andrews as an attractive destination for holidaymakers, the retired, and gentlepersons of leisure began to be more effectively exploited. Hotels sprang up, and houses, from modest to fairly grand, began to fill the open spaces between and beyond the old medieval streets, which had been preserved mainly as a result of the town languishing in something of a depression for so many years.

The boost to the economy fuelled by tourism and the arrival of more wealthy residents also stimulated the development of new grand-looking public buildings. One of the first of these was the Royal and Ancient clubhouse, which stands by what are now the first tee and the 18th green of the Old Course. In 1835, newly retired from military service, the then Major Playfair had formed a club called the Union Club, which ran a small clubhouse called the Union Parlour. Most of this club's members were also members of the Royal and Ancient.

In 1854 a new, far more substantial clubhouse opened right on the edge of the Old Course in a prominent position by the first tee. This was known as the Union Clubhouse until the clubs merged in 1877,

Did you know?

The Leuchars to St Andrews railway suffered problems linked to poor engineering work. The civil engineer responsible, Thomas Bouch, later oversaw the building of the Tay Bridge which opened in 1877. The bridge collapsed during a heavy storm on 28 December 1879, killing over seventy train passengers. There were no survivors. No one knows exactly what happened to cause the catastrophic bridge failure, but all accounts agree that the bridge was poorly designed, poorly constructed and poorly maintained.

Did you know?

When more space was needed at the Royal and Ancient, the architect James Gillespie suggested adding an additional floor to the clubhouse. These plans were initially turned down, but were realised in 1899 at a cost of £4,087, which included additional furnishings. Windows were altered to improve the views from inside the building, with a new bay window brightening up the northern elevation. Lavatories were upgraded, and a splendid wrought iron-trimmed balcony overlooking the links was installed adjacent to the new card room.

and the grand clubhouse became known as the Royal and Ancient.

The Town Hall, developed between 1858 and 1861 by the architect J Anderson Hamilton, the Grand Hotel of 1895 designed by James Munro, and Rusack's Marine Hotel designed by David Henry, completed in 1887 and extended in 1891, are just three significant buildings dating from this period which survive today. The Grand Hotel was eventually transformed into student accommodation, but it now looks set to be returned to tourists.

Rusacks survives with its grand reputation pretty much intact, despite having become a mere link in the chain of the mega-hotel business Trust Houses Forte. Its original owner, Johann Wilhelm Christof Rusack, an immigrant from Lower Saxony and a veteran of the Franco-Prussian war, started in business as an hotelier in St Andrews by trading in the newly built Abbotsford Crescent. He expanded rapidly, taking over first the Star Hotel in Market Street and then two more private hotels. In 1884 he seized an opportunity to buy land on the Links, and in 1887 the Marine Hotel opened. It immediately became the place to stay, patronised by royals and other wealthy visitors such as the Rothschild family.

Just as today, the housing market was full of surprises. A minor slump in the mid 19th century slowed down development, but by the end of the century the local paper, The St Andrews Citizen, was describing a boom in planning applications. Craftspeople did particularly well, with many a master builder eventually retiring on the strength of income derived from this transformation in the town's fortunes. In the 1890s there were at least five building yards operating in St Andrews requiring a large workforce of skilled men. Builders were working on commission and in partnership with architects on more speculative ventures. Their combined efforts resulted in the number of homes nearly doubling from 800 in the 1870s to 1574 in 1904.

In 1851 the master builder James Kennedy is known to have employed 30 masons, 12 labourers and 10 quarrymen. In 1845 Kennedy's team carried out the building work on the north wing of the United College, and his foreman on that job, John Carstairs, went on to work on the mansion West Park in Mary's Place.

ST ANDREWS FROM THE LINKS 1921 SA000416 (Courtesy of University of St Andrews Library)

The black and white postcard shows the Grand Hotel in the centre towering over the Royal and Ancient Club House on the left. The competition has all but disappeared in the stylised drawing on a promotional postcard for Rusacks Hotel (below), which seems rather larger than life.

RUSACKS MARINE HOTEL POSTCARD c1920 ZZZ03938 (Courtesy of St Andrews Preservation Trust Museum)

This was discovered when the house was later demolished to make way for the controversial Students' Union building which fills this site today. A beam bearing Carstairs's signature was revealed during demolition work. Catherine Forrest, a descendant of the Carstairs family, reveals in her excellent book about her ancestors that some of John Carstairs's descendants continue in the building trade today.

She notes that they went on to play a significant role in 20th-century building work in St Andrews. Given the controversy stirred up by any significant changes to the local

THE NORTH AND WEST WINGS OF THE UNITED COLLEGE FROM THE SOUTHEAST 1846 SA000501
(Courtesy of University of St Andrews Library)

This photograph is another Hill and Adamson calotype.

built environment, it is not surprising that she chooses not to name more contemporary relatives and their achievements.

The work proceeded without any grand plan. Playfair's drive helped open up enclosed land to create feasible building space in the centre of the town. He oversaw the joining up of the surviving medieval street pattern with a new series of streets allowing rows of terraced buildings to spring up wherever there was space, or as replacements for older decrepit buildings, but this was not part of a widely publicised or debated vision for the town's development. North and South Bell Streets were created (named after Dr Andrew Bell, the revered founded of Madras College) to connect North Street, Market Street and South Street. North and South Bell Streets still exist, though they are now named Greyfriar's Garden and Bell Street respectively.

Queens Garden running south from South Street, Gibson Place close to the Links, Playfair Terrace on North Street, and Gillespie Terrace at the western end of the Scores were all developed between 1834 and 1858. Suburban St Andrews was evolving to the west with Kennedy and Wardlaw Gardens branching from Hepburn Gardens.

Walk down Hepburn Gardens today, and you will see not just the designs but the homes of some of the people who shaped the town in the 19th century. For example, the local architect James Scott built the villas Rokeby and St Ronans at 9 and 11 Hepburn Gardens in 1894, and lived in Rokeby with his family until the First World War.

JAMES SCOTT'S HOUSES AT 9 AND 11 HEPBURN GARDENS 2005 ZZZ03922 (Shelagh Young)

These houses were built in 1894, and their design was new to St Andrews. The interesting rounded tapering chimneys were probably influenced by American styles featured in architectural journals of the day.

THE BOYS' BRIGADE HALL, KINNESSBURN ROAD 2005 ZZZ03909 (Shelagh Young)

THE BOYS' BRIGADE MEMBERSHIP CARD 1942-43
ZZZ039331 (Courtesy of St Andrews Preservation Trust Museum)

Gillespie & Scott also designed the Boys' Brigade Hall in Kinnessburn Road which opened in 1899. Christian-inspired organisations have long played a central role in the town's social life, and many would argue that they still do.

WESTERLEE, NOW PART OF WARDLAW HALL, KENNEDY GARDENS 2005
ZZZ03908 (Shelagh Young)

Rathmore, built in Kennedy Gardens in 1861 for the successful St Andrews grocer Andrew Aikman, was originally known as Rathelpie Villa. It was the work of the architect John Milne, who was also responsible for the nearby baronial-style Westerlee, now the Wardlaw Hall of Residence. Completed in 1867, Westerlee was more modern than the romantic over-the-top turrets and castellations suggest. Milne's plans relied on the latest technology in glass production to incorporate larger-than-usual windows to compensate for its north-facing site.

It would be wrong to suggest that

Did you know?

Open fires rely on drawing in large quantities of air to keep them burning strongly. Even a wealthy Victorian could not escape the cold draughts caused by winter fires sucking air from under doors, through window frames and through the floorboards. In 1851 the St Andrews architect James Milne invented a ventilation system designed to overcome this problem. His pyro-pneumatic room-grate, designed to conserve heat, won a medal at the 1874 Paris International Exhibition.

James Robert Hope

Howard Place, Hope Street and Abbotsford Crescent were three 19th-century streets built with the gentleman golfer in mind. James Robert Hope QC foresaw the need for 'gentlemen's houses', and bought parkland a little to the north of Market Street to realise his vision of a charming garden square. Work started in 1849 on a scheme which retained a central, shared garden square which is still used by today's residents. It is said that Hope's vision was inspired by Edinburgh's New Town, and the curved terraces certainly echo that style. Hope married a descendant of Sir Walter Scott, Charlotte Lockhart. As well as naming nearby Lockhart Place for his wife, Hope used the name of Scott's Borders home in naming Abbotsford Crescent. Charlotte Lockhart died in 1858, and Hope married Lady Victoria Fitzalan Howard, which provided the final name for the three streets forming his garden square development.

St Andrews evolved into a town entirely devoid of manufacturing industries. Although the service, leisure and what we now call knowledge industries have formed the backbone of the local economy for some time, the 19th century saw many local people employed in manufacturing.

Golf, as ever, was at the centre of things, with golf club making forming the mainstay of local manufacturing industry. Hugh Philip was contracted by the Society of Golfers in 1819 to undertake repairs and to provide new clubs. His assistant James Wilson eventually set up his own business too. Philip's nephew Robert Forgan inherited his uncle's business in 1856, going on to become one of St Andrews' most celebrated club makers. Forgan is credited with introducing the use of hickory for club shafts following the accidental delivery of the wrong type of wood. Forgan's workshop overlooked the Links, with a smaller factory producing cleeks (metal club heads) tucked in behind 110 Market Street. His son Thomas Forgan continued the business, which employed 150 people at its peak.

THE GOLF CLUB WORKS c1900 SA000394 (Courtesy of University of St Andrews Library)

Meanwhile Robert Wilson was working in North Street on refining iron cleek design. Innovations was needed to cope with the move from the 200-year-old featherie ball, a leather-bound sphere of pure down, to the gutta-percha ball which came into play in 1848.

This new ball posed an instant threat to the small-scale manufacturing economy of St Andrews. Although there were complexities involved in the construction of the new fangled gutta-percha balls, the skills did not match those of the leather workers employed in hand stitching the old featherie balls. This meant that almost anyone could start producing balls.

AULD DAW'S REFRESHMENT BARROW c1900 SA000373 (Courtesy of University of St Andrews Library)

David Anderson, known as Auld Daw, was a featherie ball maker before becoming senior caddy and then Keeper of the Green at St Andrews. In 1856 he set up this refreshment stall on the ninth green of the Old Course. His sons David and James went on to be expert club makers.

Early Golf Clubs

Many weird and wonderful-looking clubs from the past are on display at the British Golf Museum in St Andrews. Most would be illegal under modern golfing rules. Some were cunningly designed with short heads to clear the sides of the narrow ruts in cart and sheep tracks. Later, brass plates were added beneath the heads to cut down on wear and tear while playing off stony surfaces. The first full-time St Andrean golf club maker is thought to be James Pett, who supplied clubs to the Marquis of Montrose in 1672. King James IV commissioned a bow maker, William Mayne of Perth, to produce a set of clubs for him in 1502. In 1506 records show a handcrafted club costing one shilling (5p). This would have been formed entirely from wood. The club head would be carved from a native species of hardwood such as beech, holly, pear or apple, and the shafts from ash or the more flexible hazel. Head and shaft would be fixed with leather bindings, and few survived a complete round of golf without breaking, making it an expensive game.

The ball maker and golfer Allan Robertson was reputed to have gone round burning gutta-percha balls, so angry was he at the threat to his livelihood. By 1844 Robertson's shop was producing 2,456 balls, but he could see problems ahead. His ire extended to his business colleague Tom Morris, who broke his promise to eschew the new balls when he played in a match using gutta-percha balls. This caused a split between them. Morris went on to open his own shop producing both kinds of balls as well as clubs. Fortunately, Robertson and others were quick to work out that new balls would require innovations in club design, and also that the reduction in cost per ball would help to increase the popularity of golf. While St Andrews lost its significant place in the production of golf balls quite quickly after the gutta-percha ball came in, the production of clubs was a strength of the town for many years.

While some makers experimented with bone, metal started to be used in clubs in the 18th century, most usually inset to the face of the club to try and prevent the heads from shattering. An all-metal head was produced as early as 1750. Now old clubs are highly collectable, fetching ever higher prices at auction. 19th- and 20th-century clubs by well-known makers such as Robert Forgan and Willie Park sell for thousands of pounds. The building which housed Forgan's workshop still stands by the Links. A retail sales space for many years, the former golf club works is now supporting the St Andrews Links Trust through the sale of golfing goods and souvenirs made elsewhere.

AUCHTERLONIE GOLF CLUB ADVERTISEMENT, MADRAS COLLEGE MAGAZINE 1949
ZZZ03932 (Courtesy of St Andrews Preservation Trust Museum)

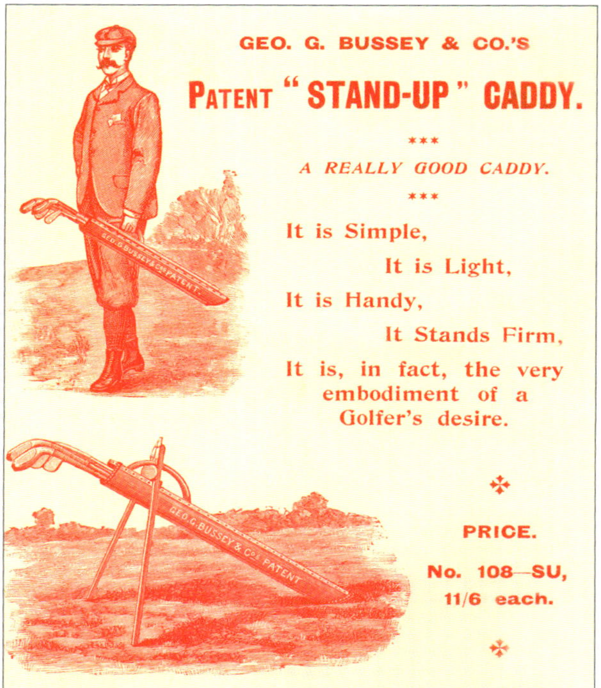

BUSSEY & CO 'STAND-UP' CADDY ADVERTISEMENT
ZZZ03940 (Courtesy of St Andrews Preservation Trust Museum)

Club making in St Andrews was continued by the Auchterlonie family until 1986. The original shop in Golf Place opened in 1935, and still trades under the Auchterlonie name selling golfing equipment. The 'stand-up' caddy has given way to ever more sophisticated and expensive devices.

Did you know?

The gutta-percha ball was an accidental discovery. The Reverend James Paterson, a missionary based in India, packed an item sent back home to St Andrews with cushioning strips of latex derived from gutta-percha. James and his brother played around with balls made from the material and realised its potential. It seems ridiculous now, but along with its superior action in flight the gutta-percha ball also impressed its users because it was more consistent in shape than the featherie and therefore rolled straight.

WILSON'S LEMONADE LABEL
ZZZ03945 (Courtesy of St Andrews Preservation Trust Museum)

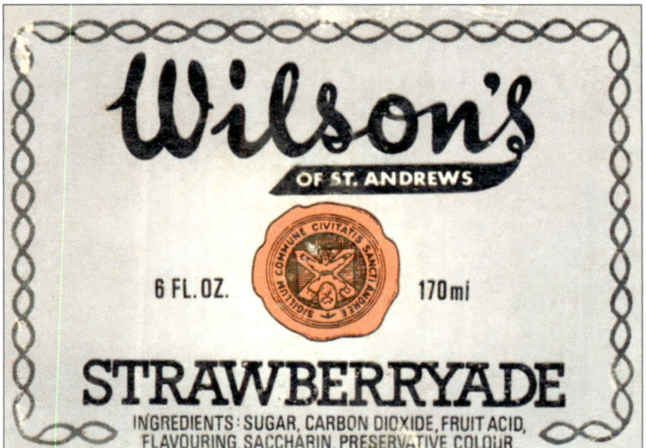

WILSON'S STRAWBERRYADE LABEL
ZZZ03946 (Courtesy of St Andrews Preservation Trust Museum)

AT THE HARBOUR 1888 SA000484
(Courtesy of University of St Andrews Library)

Along with fishing, small-scale and light industries such as brewing, an aerated water factory producing flavoured lemonades, blacksmithing, printing, joinery, building, and a continuing involvement in textiles, including a small embroidery workshop, provided employment. Service industries such as laundering grew in pace with the tourism and golfing boom, which also generated new forms of employment. For example, many fisherfolk became caddies, and eventually knowledgeable and/or highly successful competitive golfers in their own right. All this and more was sustained in part by tourism, but also by the enduring wealth of well-to-do farmers and landowners in the surrounding area.

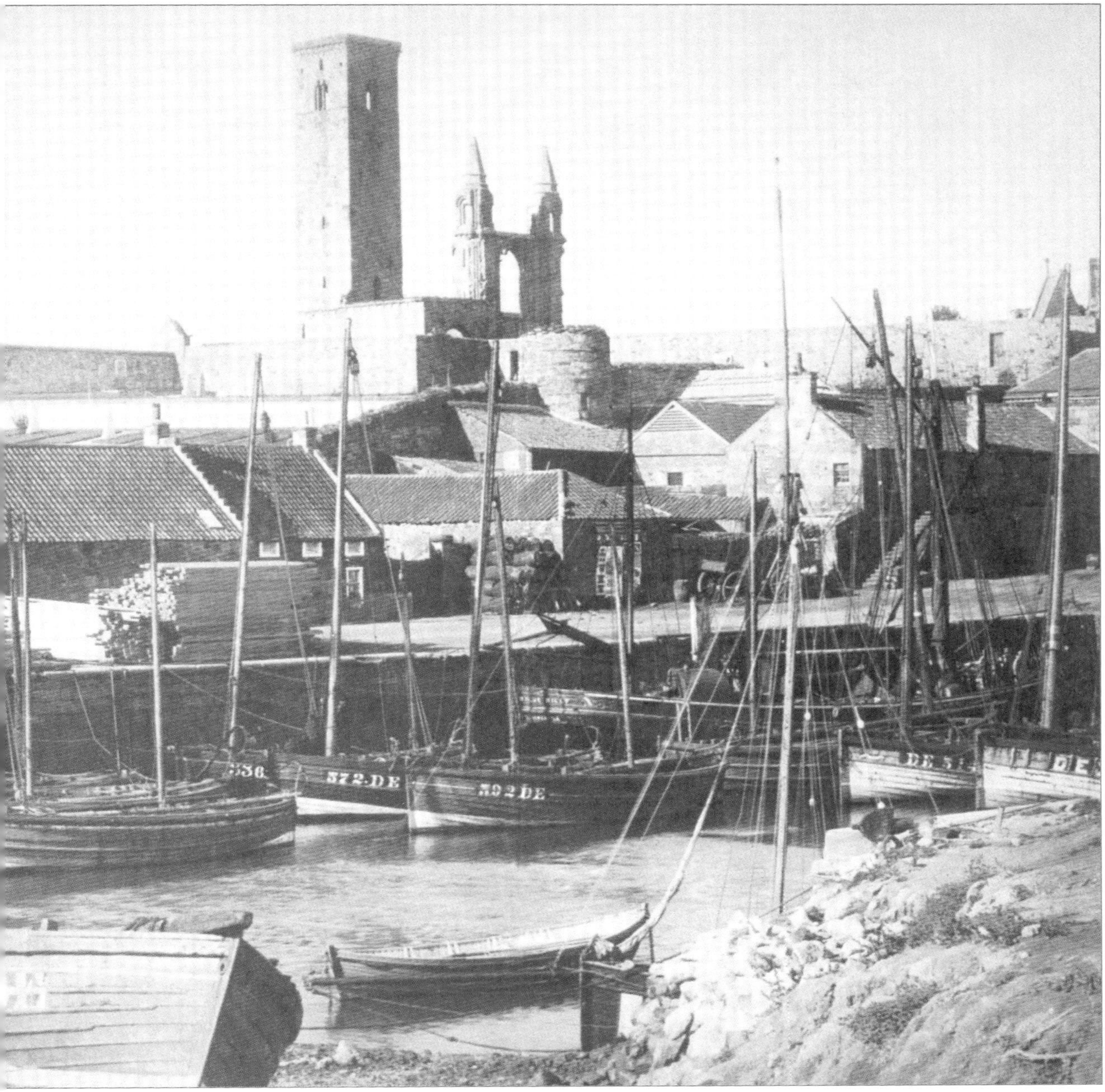

Timber stacked by the harbour suggests that the harbour continued to be used for freight even after the arrival of the railway in 1852.

Did you know?

In 1885 local fisherfolk protested at new rules on fishing recommended by a Trawling Commission. They marched to Hope Street, the home of a commission member William McIntosh, and burned an effigy. Supported by the wealthy natural historian Charles Gatty, McIntosh developed the Gatty Marine Laboratory, which opened in 1895. Its Sea Mammal Research Unit still upsets fisherfolk by supporting conservation orders which limit the hunting of seals even where fishing is affected by these natural predators.

A growing fashion for seaside holidays, with the added attraction of a chance to play golf, drove visitor numbers upwards. Opportunities for entrepreneurial types abounded. Even Victorian prudery generated jobs. The sexes were segregated at the seaside. Arrangements to protect modesty and decency were overseen by the town councillors, who declared the area around Step Rock to be suitable for male bathing and designated Castle Beach for use by women.

Bathing machines, basically sheds on wheels, which could deposit naked or modest bathers into the sea at a suitable distance from the shore, were also in use on the West Sands from the 1860s. They were described as being propelled by Amazonian-looking fishwives, who may have found the job slightly more pleasant than gutting and packing herrings.

ON THE WEST SANDS c1900 SA000392 (Courtesy of University of St Andrews Library)

ST ANDREWS FROM THE LINKS c1890 SA000488 (Courtesy of University of St Andrews Library)

Tents as well as the more unwieldy bathing machines were used for changing. Beach entertainments in the 19th and early 20th century included sandcastle building, donkey and pony rides, and musicians and performers, who often chose a religious theme.

Did you know?

Hot and cold baths for ladies, along with accommodation, were developed in 1810 on the cliff's edge close to the castle. The entrepreneur Captain Jackson used this mini-spa to capitalise on the growing trend for turning to the curative effects of sea water. In the same town where pilgrims prayed by the bones of St Andrew for a cure for what ailed them, well-to-do visitors now sought nature's cure for conditions including 'ulcers, scabs, scaled hands, itching, leprosy, corns, tumours, pains in the limbs, hydrophobia, all inflammations, all catarrhal effects, nephritis, gonorrhoea and arthritis'.

The first great golfing tournament of the modern golfing era took place in 1857 shortly after the original clubhouse building was completed. It was designed as a team event, and the play was organised into rounds by means of drawing lots. One pair of players represented each club, playing 30 holes in a knock-out competition. It was so successful that the event was scheduled for the following year, although this time it was an individual tournament open to 'all gentlemen players' who were members of any established golf club. It is a surprising fact that the Royal and Ancient neither hosted nor inaugurated the first open championship. This was held at Prestwick in 1860, and attracted just eight players who completed three rounds of a 12-hole course. By 1872 the Open Championship was truly open in the sense that players worldwide, amateur and professional, were eligible to take part; the Royal and Ancient ran it in conjunction with Prestwick and the Honourable Company of Edinburgh Golfers. They were later joined by other clubs, who shared the management of the event.

THE MONUMENT TO YOUNG TOM MORRIS, ST ANDREW'S CATHEDRAL CEMETERY 2005
ZZZ03919 (Shelagh Young)

The original trophy, a silver-decorated red leather belt, had been secured by young Tom Morris following his third win in a row. The new organisers of the Open decided on a trophy in the form of a claret jug; this, along with substantial prize money, is what golfers win today. It is sad that young Tom Morris, son of the celebrated St Andrews green keeper Tom Morris, died at the peak of his playing powers at the shockingly young age of 24. Had he lived, many suggest that he would have laid permanent claim to the claret jug too.

Club membership was not essential to the sport. Access to the links was free to everyone until 1913, when a charge to visitors of 5p a round was levied. Residents of St Andrews continued to play the course without charge until 1946, when access was restricted to those willing to pay an annual subscription. Nowadays a round on the hallowed Old Course links must be booked from September the year before one wants to play. Either that, or add your name to a ballot the day before and keep your fingers crossed that luck will deliver this once-in-a-lifetime golfing

THE TOM MORRIS GOLF SHOP OVERLOOKING THE LINKS 2005 ZZZ03916 (Shelagh Young)

opportunity at the thoroughly modern price of £115 per round in high season.

The ballot is overseen by the St Andrews Links Trust, as the Old Course continues to be owned by the people of St Andrews. The Royal and Ancient Club oversees the rules of golf worldwide, but has never owned the most famous course in the world. It nearly became the owner in 1893 when James Cheape of Strathtyrum (the man who saved the Links from the rabbit farmers) attempted to sell the land to the club for £5000.

The club's bid exceeded that of the Town Council by £500, but the council successfully lobbied Parliament to ensure that the Links returned to public ownership. When local authorities were reorganised in the 1970s, the common ownership of the Links was safeguarded by the creation of the St Andrews Links Trust.

CHAPTER FOUR

Living in the Home of Golf

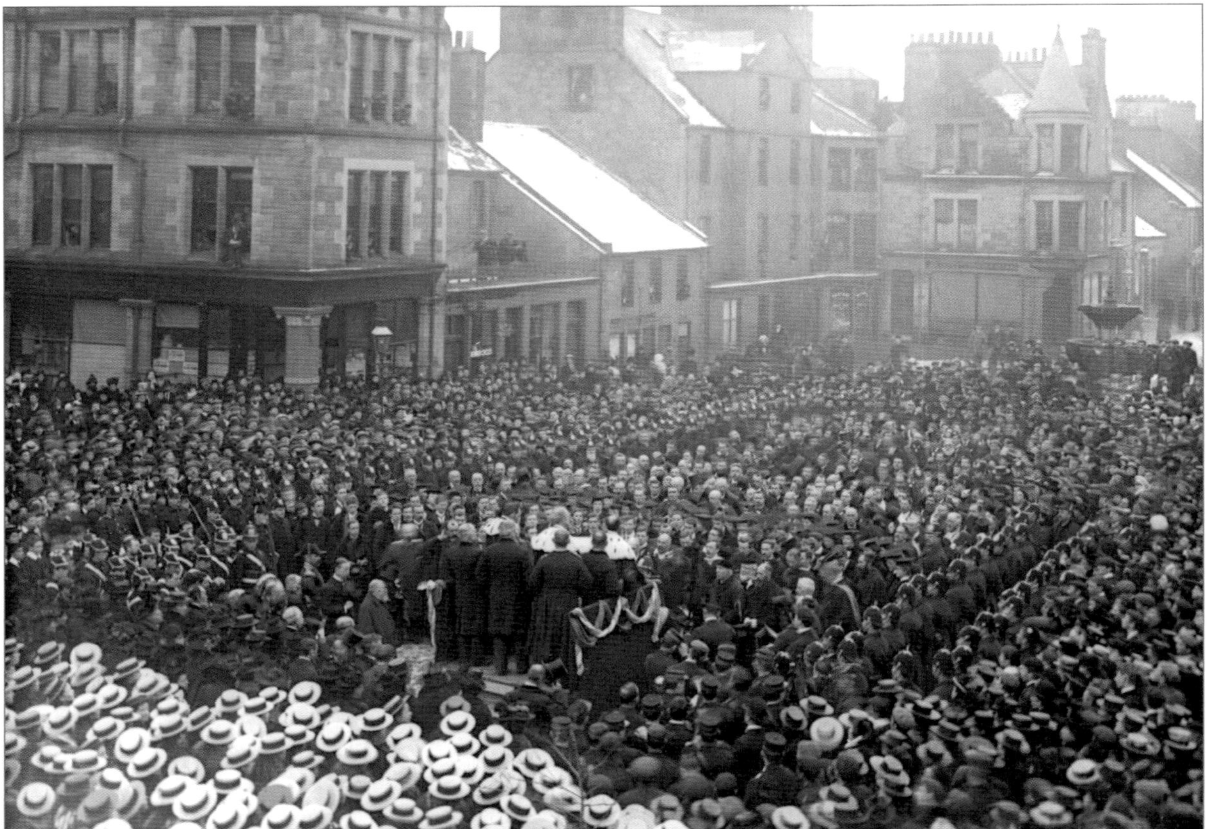

THE PROCLAMATION OF KING EDWARD VII, MARKET STREET 1901 SA000366 (Courtesy of University of St Andrews Libary)

ON 26 JANUARY 1901 St Andreans gathered at the town's traditional meeting place, the old Mercat Cross in Market Street, to hear of the death of Queen Victoria and the accession of King Edward VII. The photographs taken of the crowds gathered on that day give some indication of the growth of the town. St Andrews entered the Edwardian age at full steam. By 1914 there were 7000 people living in St Andrews, and the first decade of the 20th century saw huge developments in amenities and services designed to meet their needs.

A purpose-built hospital was created down by the Kinness Burn in what is known today as Abbey Walk. The Cottage Hospital, which opened in August 1902, replaced earlier rented facilities in Abbey Street and a hospital in Abbotsford Place partly funded by a memorial fund for Dr John Adamson. The Gibson Hospital had previously opened in a grand purpose-built Victorian building in Argyle Street in 1884 to provide care 'for the aged sick and infirm poor'. This grand Victorian building was the work of the architect David Henry. It is still there, nowadays operating as a retirement home.

GIBSON HOSPITAL, ARGYLE STREET 2005 ZZZ03928 (Shelagh Young)

GIBSON HOSPITAL PLAQUE 2005 ZZZ03911 (Shelagh Young)

Did you know?

The Freddy Tait memorial ward in the Cottage Hospital was named for the admired golfer Freddy Tait, who was killed fighting in the Boer War on 7 February 1900. His mother helped fund the £3000 cost of the hospital. Some donations came with strings attached. For many years the needs of golfers, caddies and soldiers from the Black Watch took priority over other patients.

Fife's best-known philanthropist, the steel magnate Andrew Carnegie, also made gifts to St Andrews. He was rector of the university from 1901 to 1907; as well as giving a new organ for the university chapel in 1904, a gymnasium the following year, and a university library extension in 1908, he also paid for a recreation park and pavilion. His greatest gift to Scottish university education came in the form of the Carnegie Trust for the Universities of Scotland, endowed with 10 million US dollars.

By 1910 St Andrews University was described as having 'a larger number of students' and as doing 'a greater variety of work in all departments of study than at any period in its history.' Some of this success can certainly be attributed to the funds provided by Carnegie.

A growing population led to greater attention being paid to safety as well as health. The comparatively wealthy community supported early modernisation such as the introduction of electric lighting in 1909. Fire had been a problem during the heyday of timber-built homes, and as early as 1700 the local authorities had ordered the provision of fire buckets made from 'a good hide of inglish uppers'. A manual fire pump (which had failed to

save the Woodburn Sawmill from burning to the ground in 1863) had been superseded by an improved manual pump - it at least had enough buckets, so that pans need not be borrowed at the scene as had previously been the case. Fortunately, in 1901 struggling fundraising efforts were boosted when a brand new steam fire engine was donated by local man Major Donald Lindsay Carnegie of Playfair Terrace. He also donated an ambulance in 1906, as well as x-ray equipment to the hospital.

THE STEAM FIRE ENGINE 1 JUNE 1901 SA000368 (Courtesy of University of St Andrews Library)

Church building, church renovation, and the development of gathering places such as church halls had been a significant feature of the Victorian era and continued through the turn of the century. St Andrew's on Queen's Terrace replaced the earlier North Street Episcopal church when it was consecrated in 1877. Hope Park Church at St Mary's Place was built in 1864, with a church hall following in 1900. The 1843 Martyr's Church in North Street was born out of the Free Church movement. A spire and redesigned frontage were added to the building in 1851. Plans for a total redevelopment were stymied by the First World War, but they went ahead in 1925, with a church hall following in 1934. The stained glass seen today dates from this period. The Baptist church on South Street by Rose Lane is still housed in a building remodelled in 1901, although the foundation of a Baptist congregation in St Andrews goes back to at least 1841.

HOLY TRINITY CHURCH c1900 SA000372 (Courtesy of University of St Andrews Library)

HOLY TRINITY CHURCH 2005 ZZZ03912 (Shelagh Young)

Holy Trinity used its central location to good effect when promoting St Andrews 2005 Fair Trade Fortnight, an anti-poverty initiative that was widely supported by local businesses, community groups and other churches.

Holy Trinity Church, on the corner of Church Street and South Street, perhaps has the finest features of all the town's churches which are still in use today. The tower dates from 1412. The rest of the church was remodelled between 1907 and 1909, with many earlier elements retained. The contents and fabric of the church tell us something about the history of the town.

The John Knox Porch is a reminder of Knox's involvement in the ransacking of the cathedral which followed his preaching here in 1559. There is a beautifully carved marble tomb and monument in memory of Archbishop Sharp, a royalist who was murdered in 1679 by the Covenanters - they objected to Charles II restoring bishops and royal control over the church.

The splendid west window was a gift from the women of the congregation in 1914, an indication of just how wealthy some St Andreans had become.

The quiet return of Roman Catholicism to St Andrews was marked by small-scale home-based masses until a church was opened in 1885. This church was St James's, a corrugated iron creation known locally as 'the tin tabernacle'; it was replaced by a more sturdy building in 1910.

The replacement was the first independent commission for the Edinburgh architect Reginald Fairlie, and its prominent location on the Scores overlooking Step Rock and the Witches Pool ensured that the building commanded attention. It is recorded as the last major building in St Andrews to be completely constructed from the locally quarried Strathkinness stone. Among other commissions, Fairlie also went on to oversee the renovations of Queen Mary's House in 1927 and the restoration of St Salvator's Chapel in 1931.

WITCH LAKE 1887 SA000506 (Courtesy of University of St Andrews Library)

ST JAMES'S CHURCH OCTOBER 1909 SA000383 (Courtesy of University of St Andrews Library)

Here we see St James's Church, known as 'the tin tabernacle', in its original position on the Scores overlooking Witch Lake (see photograph on page 82), and being moved to a new location to make way for the new stone church (above).

Did you know?

The first modern Episcopal church in North Street was consecrated in 1825. Forty-five years later it was replaced by the current church, which stands in Queen's Terrace. In 1870 the North Street church was purchased by the Free Church for £130 and shipped, stone by stone, to be re-erected in Buckhaven on the south coast of Fife.

THE UNVEILING OF THE WAR MEMORIAL 23 SEPTEMBER 1922
SA000367 (Courtesy of University of St Andrews Library)

The town's war memorial was unveiled at the top of North Street in 1922 by Field-Marshal Haig of Bemersyde (on the right of photograph SA000367); it lists over 80 men from St Andrews who were killed in the Great War.

It was updated later to include the smaller number of men lost in the Second World War. Overall, these conflicts trod lightly on the town. Men from the Lancashire Hussars and the Highland Cycle Brigade were stationed at St Andrews during the First World War, but the main impact was economic. Media censorship ensured that the average St Andrean was well protected from the carnage happening so far away.

SOLDIERS ON GUARD c1915 SA000391 (Courtesy of University of St Andrews Library)

A group of the Lancashire Hussars on guard in St Andrews during the First World War.

Did you know?

St Andrews-born life peer Lord Jo Grimond (1913-1993) told a story about the German Wilhelm (Willie) Rusack who founded Rusack's Marine Hotel. He wrote that the elderly Rusack, a naturalised British citizen, was suspected of spying during the First World War: it was alleged that he had been signalling to German submarines from the hotel roof. There is no record of his internment as an enemy alien, so presumably he was considered innocent. The photograph shows Willie Rusack in the driver's seat in happier days.

FOUR GENTLEMEN GOLFERS 1904 SA000369 (Courtesy of University of St Andrews Library)

In August 1939 the German airship 'Graf Zeppelin II' cruised within sight of St Andrews only a month before war was officially declared. It was chased away by two RAF Spitfires operating out of RAF Leuchars, a hint of the air battles to come. The 'blitz' of St Andrews was very small-scale, though none the less frightening for residents, twelve of whom lost their lives. On one terrifying night, 25 October 1940, four bombs fell. One destroyed a cottage in Alison Place, another fell in Westburn Lane damaging the Bute Building, and another at St Mary's College, damaging the University Library and many books. The fourth fell near Kinnessburn, and reportedly caused little damage. Another bomb fell at a later date destroying a home at the Pipeland Road end of Nelson Street.

AIR RAID DAMAGE, NELSON STREET 1940 SA000511 (Courtesy of University of St Andrews Library)

The press photographer George M Cowie donated his photographs to the university. They cover a period from the 1930s to his death in 1982. Together with the work of John Fairweather, the collection provides wonderful insights into the modern social history of St Andrews.

Enemy Aliens?

John Di Folco's Italian grandparents came to St Andrews in 1909. They ran a fish and chip shop and grocer's. In 1951 his parents opened St Andrews' first delicatessen, with stock from Edinburgh's renowned Valvona & Crolla. They made a good living selling such rare (in 1950s Scotland) exotics as red peppers, panettone and olive oil to other local Italian families. But the future had not always looked so rosy. In the Second World War John's grandfather, father and uncle were all detained as enemy aliens pending tribunals which would decide whether or not they posed a threat to national security. Members of the St Andrews-based Jannetta and Palumbo families were also detained, first at Edinburgh's Saughton Jail and later on the Isle of Wight. Letters home from the detainees show a touching faith in British fairness and bureaucracy. It is perhaps understandable that the British Government was not so trusting. This letter from the Home Office to the local Conservative MP James Henderson Stewart refuses to review the detention of Carmino Jannetta, who is described as a person of 'hostile origin and associations'.

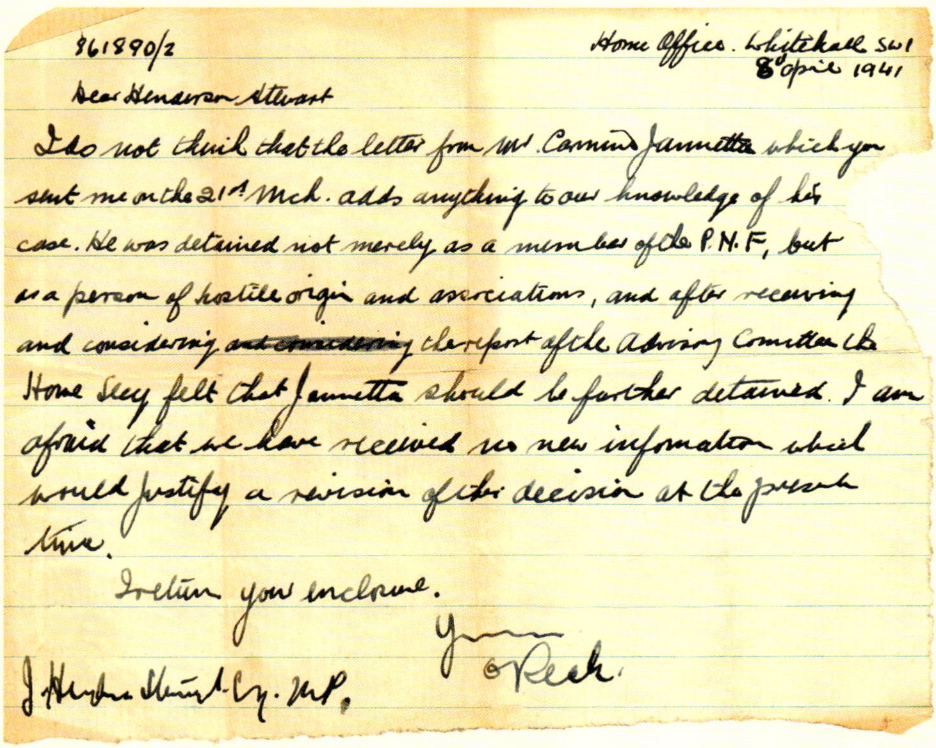

861890/2

Home Office. Whitehall SW1
8 April 1941

Dear Henderson Stewart

I do not think that the letter from Mr. Carmino Jannetta which you sent me on the 21st Mch. adds anything to our knowledge of his case. He was detained not merely as a member of the P.N.F, but as a person of hostile origin and associations, and after receiving and considering ~~and considering~~ the report of the Advisory Committee the Home Secy felt that Jannetta should be further detained. I am afraid that we have received no new information which would justify a revision of this decision at the present time.

I return your enclosure.

Yours
Peak.

J. Henderson Stewart Esq. MP.

A LETTER FROM THE HOME OFFICE REGARDING THE DETENTION OF CARMINO JANNETTA 8 APRIL 1941 ZZZ03942 (Courtesy of St Andrews Preservation Trust Museum)

Golfing continued to grow as an attraction throughout this period, but it was not the only growth area for leisure activity. The annual Lammas Market had featured popular 'kinematographic' tents showing silent movies as early as 1890. In 1909 St Andrews gained La Scala, known to locals as the Pamie Ramie. This James Street building became the town's first cinema, showing films on Sunday nights with tickets at a penny each, as well as hosting dances and roller skating. The building had traditionally been busy on a Sunday, as it was actually the old St James's Church, the Tin Tabernacle, which had been dragged in three segments to its new site by a steam-powered traction engine. It is said that the audience had to sing a hymn before each film performance to make the gathering legal. There were also film screenings at the Town Hall.

A purpose-built picture house followed in 1913 on North Street. Called the Cinema House, it soon attracted large audiences, and occasionally jazzed up proceedings by providing full orchestration to accompany the silent films. In 1929, following the retirement of the original cinema manager Jim Reid, it was equipped with new projectors and speakers. Audiences could now enjoy the new 'talkies' and regular newsreels without having to be able to read the captions. However a competitor emerged in North Street when the New Picture House opened in 1931 complete with comparatively luxurious facilities. A large café, function suite and interior foyer with ticket office and shop made this a popular space for socialising.

THE NEW PICTURE HOUSE PROGRAMME 1935
ZZZ03933 (Courtesy of St Andrews Preservation Trust Museum)

In the 1940s a St Andrews film society was set up. The management of the New Picture House agreed to allows its premises to be used on Sunday afternoons and evenings for the club's weekly term-time screenings. Betty Willsher, who has written books on the history of the town and its people, vividly remembers cycling home after watching a distressing film, possibly a screening of Ingmar Bergman's 'Au Revoir Les Enfants', with tears streaming down her face - tears which she feared would freeze in the frosty night air.

THE CINEMA HOUSE GOLDEN JUBILEE POSTER 1963
ZZZ03939 (Courtesy of St Andrews Preservation Trust Museum)

The Cinema House became a victim of the hard times that hit the cinema industry in the 1970s. Closed with just one day's notice in December 1979, the Cinema House went to the great auditorium in the sky while still under the 51-year-long management of Jack Humphries. He was well respected as a long-serving town councillor and member of the St Andrews Golf Club, but perhaps best loved for the welcome he gave to so many filmgoers through the years. A fragment of the now demolished Cinema House survives. The stained glass sign from above the door is kept safe in the Town Museum in Kinburn Park. In contrast, the New Picture House is still going strong. It is currently trading as a two-screen cinema in its original building. Its crow-stepped gabled design makes it look more like a 17th-century Scottish merchant's house than a classic Art Deco picture palace typical of British cinema in this period.

Provision for outdoor pursuits, despite the frequent dreich winter days and the unavoidable summer haars (thick sea mists), was also increasing in the Edwardian era. A fancy wrought iron bandstand for outdoor concerts went up on the Bow Butts in 1905. Music is still played here in summertime supported by the local and the community councils, although there is the occasional hiccup. Apparently when the Clackmannan Brass Band was engaged to play in August 2004, a St Andrews-based police officer was unable to direct them to the bandstand as he didn't know there was one. He tried sending them to the Cupar bandstand instead.

Did you know?

St Andrews' own brass band was formed in 1879. The band was given smart blue and yellow outfits by Provost Milton. In addition to summer concerts, the band played at the Lammas Market and for ice skaters. The band's demise was attributed in the newspaper to 'an invention called wireless which dispensed dance music', but since it happened during the First World War the availability of fit young male players is a more likely explanation.

Donkey rides were introduced to the beaches as early as the 18th century, and brightly costumed troupes of pierrots first appeared in 1891. Musicians strolled along the beaches attracting large crowds. Open-air productions of plays with a religious theme were popular along the East Bents, and tourists were entertained with productions that emphasised the town's rich religious heritage.

Swimming facilities made a great leap forward in 1903 with the creation of a 300ft-long seawater pool in what had long been a popular bathing spot at the foot of the distinctive Step Rock. Swimming galas were held at the Step Rock Pool almost from its opening. An amateur swimming club was formed in 1928, with cinema manager Jack Humphries as its first president. An amateur lifeguard corps was set up, and in 1938 it launched its first patrol boat, a sleek white-painted cutter that went to the aid of swimmers and boating parties in distress. The brand-new boat cost £9, and was powered by six oarsmen. Although the Step Rock Swimming Pool had started life as a male only swimming venue, women started using it from 1904. New changing cubicles built in the 1930s helped them keep their modesty intact. Galas eventually included a bathing belle competition alongside more strenuous competitive events such as water polo, diving and straightforward swimming races.

David Gourlay, who was raised in South Street and now lives in North Street, joined the Step Rock Swimming Club in 1930 at the age of eight. He recalls being taken along by a friend and being 'joined up' by his mother despite not being sure about the attractions of the freezing cold waters. His swimming lessons were a success despite the inevitable numbing of his body parts, and he fondly remembers the pre-war club as being very competitive. Gourlay was never a regular daily swimmer like the renowned grocer Provost Aikman, who at the age of 76 in the 1920s was still swimming all year round. Gourlay only remembers braving the waters between April and September, the official summer opening period of the pool.

After Second World War Service in the RAF, David Gourlay returned to become a committee member and was later awarded life membership of the club. His involvement lasted until the 1970s, when the pool with its grand-looking 1930s concrete pavilion needed expensive repairs. The Town Council declined to spend what was needed, and the pool closed in 1976. It reopened in 1989 as the Sea Life Centre, an aquarium which currently features seals, sharks, piranha and

THE STEP ROCK SWIMMING POOL 1935 SA000398 (Courtesy of University of St Andrews Library)

THE STEP ROCK c1900 SA000393 (Courtesy of University of St Andrews Library)

starfish amongst its living exhibits.

Gourlay's story might have been very different had he followed the paternal line in sporting activities. His father and grandfather were both keen golfers, the latter having been a professional golfer. This interest in golf was transmitted to the young Gourlay, although, he says, not the skill.

He remembers his father making miniature clubs for him at about the same time he took up swimming. Although he played golf for many years, and took part in competitions organized by the Burgh School (which he attended prior to Madras School), swimming and in later years rifle shooting were the sports in which he excelled.

Did you know?

The West Sands were reputedly a favourite landing site for recreational flyers bound to and from the nearby Leuchars airfield because fuel was easily accessible. Leuchars served as an air training school in 1916, becoming RAF Leuchars in 1920, and the first of several civil air displays took place over the West Sands in 1919. Before that, motorcycle and motor racing had begun on the beach. Motorcycle rallies were held from 1908 up until the 1950s.

THE WEST SANDS, NATIONAL AVIATION DAY DISPLAY 1932 SA000510 (Courtesy of University of St Andrews Library)

ST ANDREWS FROM THE WEST SANDS 1936 SA000395 (Courtesy of University of St Andrews Library)

St. Andrews Motor Club
(AFFILIATED TO S.A.C.U.)

OFFICIAL PROGRAMME
FOR
SAND RACING
THURSDAY, 9th AUGUST 1934
at 7 p.m.
in aid of the Sir James Mackenzie Institute.

OFFICIALS

Clerk of Course	Mr. A. H. STEELE
Starter	A. H. STEELE
Lap Scorers	R. B. CARNEGIE, G. CHRISTIE
Pit Marshal	A. ANDERSON
Flagsman	S. SPENCER
Judges	W. DUNCAN, McKAY BRYANT, W. K. ELLIOT
Marshals	W. R. BROWN, S. JAQUES, S. GREIG
Secretary	H. A. HAXTON, Rokeby St. Andrews

PROGRAMME - THREEPENCE

ST ANDREWS MOTOR CLUB, SAND RACING OFFICIAL PROGRAMME 1934
ZZZ03937 (Courtesy of St Andrews Preservation Trust Museum)

A PACKAGE ADDRESSED TO GORDON CHRISTIE CONTAINING BIKE TRANSFERS 1951 ZZZ03941 (Courtesy of St Andrews Preservation Trust Museum)

The Christie brothers, Jack and Andrew, started sand racing at St Andrews after opening their cycle manufacturing business and shop in 1908. Andrew's son Gordon retired from his cycle shop in 1975. He has subsequently been very active in the community, becoming an invaluable source of information for historians.

Between the wars St Andrews continued to grow in terms of culture, architecture and the economy. The Byre Theatre, now housed in a beautiful if controversial purpose-built space in Abbey Street, was founded in a former cow shed in 1933. A ship's ladder, bought from a Fife dockyard, formed the only access from stage to dressing rooms, and the audience sat in 74 second-hand seats donated by Jack Humphries of the Cinema House. The founder Alex Paterson started as a playwright, and it was traditional for the Byre's season to always open with one of his plays. He stayed on as chairman of the Byre Theatre Board until his death in 1989, and successfully led the theatre through several relocations, planning battles and funding crises.

BYRE THEATRE LEAFLET c1970 ZZZ03934
(Courtesy of St Andrews Preservation Trust Museum)

BYRE THEATRE PROGRAMME 1979
ZZZ03935 (Courtesy of St Andrews Preservation Trust Museum)

This leaflet (left) shows the second Byre Theatre in its first purpose-built space a few metres away from its original Abbey Street location. The programme is for the Christmas 1979 production of 'Jack and the Beanstalk', with adult seats priced at just £1.60.

The inter-war years also saw the foundations laid for today's conservative approach to development in the town. Throughout the first half of the 20th century, well meaning town planning and housing acts strongly encouraged redevelopment and the demolition of slum housing. Some felt that this placed the unique fabric and nature of St Andrews under threat. Concern can be dated to 1919 and a housing act known as the Addison Act. This was designed to ensure an adequate supply of housing for working-class people; for the first time, it offered local authorities a central government subsidy for housing development. Poverty had not disappeared despite relatively boom times in St Andrews, and better quality housing was desperately needed. In 1919, a hundred inhabited houses surveyed were deemed to be unfit for human habitation. A municipal scheme of 68 new houses paved the way for later developments. Between 1920 and 1929 an impressive 290 houses were built south of the Kinness Burn. In this period grants became available for slum clearance, but St Andrews was slow to take up the offer. In 1924 the council actually refused permission for a demolition order on an admittedly unfit property at 159 South Street on the grounds that there was too great a need for housing.

Nevertheless, the pressure to clear slum housing and the financial incentives for so doing caused alarm. In 1937 the St Andrews Preservation Trust was founded with the remit of securing 'the preservation of the amenities and historical character of St Andrews and its neighbourhood'. The Trust is now most obviously active in efforts to prevent a creeping suburbanisation of the town, for example through fighting to secure the all-round protection of a green belt. However, in 1937 a desire to protect the existing vernacular architecture was their primary concern. The possibility of losing virtually all the oldest domestic dwellings loomed large in 1933 when 21 buildings were cleared, including the remarkable double-decker house at the corner of Union Street and Market Street.

At first, new building was mostly confined to the outskirts of town. The tenth new housing scheme in 1934 saw 120 houses built on sites between the current Lamond Drive and Largo Road, and a further 82 new builds were agreed in 1936. By the time the Preservation Trust was formed, many town centre properties had been condemned and were boarded up. Flats for the elderly built in the 1950s in Baker Lane signified a defeat for

Did you know?

Tenants of run-down properties were reluctant to move because rent for new housing was £12 to £14 a year in comparison with around £10 paid in the slums. Council officials were keen on the social improvement that seemed to go along with relocation. They made patronising remarks about slum dwellers; for example, a report to the council noted a marked improvement 'not only in their behaviour but also their appearance' on transfer to municipal housing.

THE DOUBLE-DECKER HOUSE, MARKET STREET POST 1910 SA000357 (Courtesy of University of St Andrews Library)

Here we see the lost double-decker house and its eventual replacement, one of many modern university buildings in the centre of St Andrews.

THE BUCHANAN BUILDING, MARKET STREET c1977 SA000425 (Courtesy of University of St Andrews Library)

Did you know?

Blacksmith Ed Harvey's daughter Pat still lives in Bruce Street, part of the new municipal housing provided in the 1940s. Ed Harvey ran his own smithy, Greenside Works, after working in the Hamilton's smithy at West Port and for Gillespie's garage. From shoeing the beach donkeys he moved on to specialising in decorative ironwork. He made the east and west gates of University Hall as well as railings outside Holy Trinity Church and decorative metal trees in the greenhouses at the botanic gardens. His most well-known work was an iron harbour bridge, designed by Pat's aero-engineer brother, which was replaced only recently.

the Preservation Trust, which failed to save several houses in the street. However, James Scott, the architect son of the Gillespie and Scott partner of the same name, championed restoration with work on property intended for his own use in North Street. He and others spread the restoration bug, and some intriguing properties with their crow-stepped gables, medieval stones, inscribed marriage lintels and outdoor staircases survive intact.

It is perhaps not surprising that when Betty Willsher came up to the university from her home in Durham in 1933 she remembers a more pleasant town than contemporary housing reports described. The cab she took from the station was horse-drawn, and her destination in Kennedy Gardens was close to the impressive Rathelpie (now Rathmore) Villa built for Andrew Aikman, grocer and provost. She describes the station as being beautifully decorated with flowers and shell designs. It is interesting to wonder what visitors to the cathedral ruins subsequently thought as they passed through less affluent areas, or if they even noticed the slum housing prevalent near the town's most famous ancient attraction.

Betty Willsher

Betty Willsher graduated in psychology, and then worked in a day nursery for dockers' children in Wapping. She saw the damaging effects of poverty at first hand. After the Second World War she returned to St Andrews to start her own nursery, at first in the Lade Braes and later in Argyle Street. She was a trailblazing single parent businesswoman who later worked with young children in care and in schools in poorer parts of Fife. She is passionate about the needs of all young people, and full of praise for fellow St Andreans such as Pat Harvey and her father the late blacksmith Ed Harvey, who set up a youth club in St Andrews in the 60s. Many adults have fond memories of the Ichthus Youth Club which inherited the disused railway station in 1969 and remained there until a new centre was opened in 1971.

A positive legacy of the Second World War was the arrival of Polish soldiers, many of whom stayed to make St Andrews their permanent home. 17,000 exiled troops arrived in the UK following the fall of France in June 1940. In the east of Scotland their task was coastal defence. When General Sikorski, Commander in Chief of the Polish forces in Britain, and Prime Minister Winston Churchill made a joint tour of inspection in October 1940, they came to St Andrews. All home-based troops were experiencing equipment shortages at the time, but Churchill was reportedly so impressed by the Poles of St Andrews that he ordered that they be the first to receive more tanks, guns and ammunition. A bust of Sikorski can be found in Kinburn Park.

Maryisa Denyer was born in wartime St Andrews. Her Polish father Michael Zamora met and married her mother Emily Pinder following his dramatic escape via Hungary and France. He was stationed in Stirling on the day of her birth in 1944, and she still has the telegram announcing her arrival. Her father took part in the D-Day landings and she knows that he was with the liberating troops who saw the horrors of the

GENERAL SIKORSKI, WINSTON CHURCHILL AND MRS CHURCHILL AT THE WEST SANDS 1940
SA000489 (Courtesy of University of St Andrews Library)

MARYISA DENYER (NEE ZAMORA) WITH HER PARENTS EMILY AND MICHAEL 1944
ZZZ03903 (Courtesy of Maryisa Denyer)

MICHAEL ZAMORA AND COLLEAGUES c1940 ZZZ03904
(Courtesy of Maryisa Denyer)

Michael Zamora (third from left) stands outside one of the Polish Army billets, the Atholl Hotel. Tad Kuharski, on his left, also stayed in St Andrews after the war. He followed the local tradition, and became an accomplished photographer as well as an artist and businessman.

concentration camp at Belsen at first hand. Michael Zamora was a trained hairdresser, but he first returned to civvy street as an employee at the Guardbridge Mill. He then worked for twelve years as caretaker at the extravagant-looking turreted Westerlee, or Wardlaw Hall as it is now known, in Kennedy Gardens, before setting up his own barber's shop. Maryisa says that her school friends at the time thought she lived in a castle.

Michael died in 2001 at the age of 84, not long after he retired from his business at 134 South Street. His customers included Sir Sean Connery, the humanitarian campaigner Terry Waite, and the US author James Michener, who sent Zamora a copy of one of his books inscribed 'To the most gracious barber I've met in many years'. The shop still trades, but under a new name, 'The Barber's Pole', a pun which pays homage to Zamora.

Today there is a colourful mosaic expressing the thanks of Polish soldiers for the hospitality of the people of St Andrews on the west-facing wall of the Town Hall. The Scottish-Polish Society, which was set up in April 1941 with the aim of promoting good relations between host communities and the Poles, was clearly a success.

However, Maryisa thinks she knows why the younger female St Andreans were fond of the Poles: they were often described as 'dashing'. She recalls her father as being a keen dancer with impeccable manners whose party piece, a table-slapping version of the Pennsylvania Polka, was usually accompanied by a 'wodka' (vodka) or two.

THE POLISH MOSAIC, THE TOWN HALL 2005
ZZZ03907 (Shelagh Young)

Maryisa has fond memories from her teenage years of jiving and drinking Coca-Cola in the Red Gown Café, a venue set up in South Street by her father's friend and compatriot, the artist Tad Kuharski. She credits Tad with taking some of the fascinating photos she has of her father in wartime, which include shots of Sir Winston Churchill, General Sikorski and King George VI on their visit to St Andrews.

After the war St Andrews resumed its place on the tourist map, with golf tourism growing ever more rapidly. General Eisenhower played his first round of golf in St Andrews in 1946, and since then a steady stream of well known faces has played at least one of the growing number of courses. Bing Crosby, Sir Sean Connery, Danny Kaye and former US President Bill Clinton have all played at St Andrews - and we should not forget the controversy caused by £32,000 worth of air travel arrangements made when former Captain of the Royal and Ancient Golf Club Prince Andrew wanted to squeeze in an extra round of golf in 2004. The Guardian reported that a cost-effective alternative might have been a hire car, with two round trips costing a mere £178.80 including petrol. Perhaps the prince knew something The Guardian journalist did not about how much concern there is today about traffic congestion in St Andrews.

DANNY KAYE TEEING OFF AT THE OLD COURSE 1952 SA000508 (Courtesy of University of St Andrews Library)

CROWDS STUDY THE HEADER BOARDS IN THE BOW BUTTS 1945 SA000509 (Courtesy of University of St Andrews Library)

Facilities have developed over the years. The Old Course was joined by the New Course, laid out by the celebrated green keeper Old Tom Morris and opened in 1895. The Jubilee followed in 1897, then the Eden in 1914, which was subsequently made available for Sunday golfing in 1945. The Balgove, a small nine-hole course deemed suitable for children, opened in 1972, and in 1993 the 18-hole Strathtyrum was opened, along with a redesigned Balgove and a new golf practice centre. This brought the number of 18-hole courses in the town up to five, making it Europe's largest golfing centre.

Since 1974 the operation and maintenance of all these courses has been the responsibility of the St Andrews Links Trust. This was formed in response to plans for local government reorganisation and to safeguard public ownership of the Links. The Trust subsequently opened two non-membership clubhouses to cater for visitors: the Links Clubhouse opened in 1995 and the Eden in 2000. The other membership clubs such as the Royal and Ancient, a new British Golf Museum on Bruce Embankment, together with numerous shops supplying equipment and souvenirs to the golfing enthusiast, clustered mainly around Golf Place; and the fringes of the Links, plus numerous hotels, some with golfing themed rooms, completes the golfing holiday package which is modern-day St Andrews.

There are some residents who have resisted the lure of the little white ball. Ann Cantley came to teach at Madras College in May

1955, and while she fell sufficiently in love with the town to stay on after retirement, she finds plenty to do without resorting to golf. Miss Cantley, as she is always addressed by former pupils, is remembered by Maryisa Denyer (who started at Madras in 1957) as 'one of the best teachers' she ever had. Miss Cantley remembers that it was not hard to shine at first in a school mainly staffed by people who appeared to be 'on their last legs'. She remembers a dingy environment and doddering staff, but chuckles at the memory of the roof blowing off the brand-new staff room when the new school buildings opened in Kilrymont Road in 1967. The original building, now much extended, is still going strong, having survived the same gale intact. She retired from the role of Assistant Rector in 1984, and has since been active in the Community Council and other voluntary activities.

Ann Cantley was born in 1928, which, she reminded me, was the year in which women achieved full suffrage. Her teaching career spanned a period of great social and political change for women. She could certainly count herself as something of a role model in the process of, in her own words, 'girls coming to the fore'. She humorously refers to what she calls her 'active feminist phase', which included criticism of the men-only membership rule of the famous St Andrews Burns Club. Formed following the centenary of Burns's birth on 25 January 1759 by fourteen gentlemen of the town, the club meets every Burns night for a traditional supper. The club has been awarding an annual citizenship award since 1983.

The St Andrews Society, formed in 1981, reflects a more modern St Andrews. Its objectives are those of celebrating Scottish people and culture, of marking St Andrews Day, and making links with Scots visiting St Andrews. More than twenty years on, the society coordinates extensive annual celebrations on and around 30 November; these have included talks, walks, lunches, breakfasts at the Byre Theatre, and the publication of history booklets. In the past nine years these activities have evolved and expanded to fill a St Andrews Week festival with ceilidhs, drama, art exhibitions and an impressive firework display.

At the VE Day 50th anniversary commemorative parade organised by the Community Council in 1995, evidence of this outward, welcoming focus was provided by the presence of an American student bearing the Stars and Stripes alongside a St Andrean proudly carrying the Saltire. Scouts marched with veterans of the Royal British Legion, and children from Langlands Primary School dressed as evacuees carrying gas masks and little suitcases. The weather on the day was showery, an improvement on the town's 1977 Silver Jubilee celebrations. Then, street party-goers retired to community halls, and young girls stood to attention at the end of the parade looking more like a pack of drowned rats than a Brownie pack. The weather was also unkind to sand yachters that year. Windy St Andrews should have been the ideal venue for the 1977 Silver Jubilee Open Sand Yachting Championships. Unfortunately, the event was becalmed at Easter, and again when it was rescheduled to May. At least the annual Donkey Derby, run in Cockshaugh Park since 1975, went ahead.

The above-average number of events, pageants and parades held in this vibrant town continue to thrive despite the weather. One of

BAD WEATHER ON SILVER JUBILEE DAY 1977
SA000494 (Courtesy of University of St Andrews Library)

these is the annual Kate Kennedy Day procession in spring, organised by the university's Kate Kennedy Club to celebrate some of the great women and men of the town and the university.

The modern tradition dates back to 1926, although the celebration is thought to have evolved earlier in honour of Catherine, daughter of the 15th-century Bishop Kennedy. The event raised £30 16s 6d for the Cottage Hospital in 1926, and it still continues successfully to raise funds for good causes. One of the distinguishing features of the parade is that men always play the female characters. Some famous faces have been caught on camera in this annual cross-dressing spectacular. The Fife-born leading businessman and former Chairman of British Rail Sir Bob Reid looked particularly good in plaits when, as a student at St Andrews University in 1953, he played the young Kate Kennedy complete with a bridal-style bouquet.

For a town with so much to celebrate, and so many ways of doing it, the new Millennium appears to have been greeted in a relatively

BOB REID AS KATE KENNEDY 1953
SA000512 (Courtesy of University of St Andrews Library)

modest fashion. A family ceilidh was held in the Victory Memorial Hall organised by the Step Rock Swimming Club, and around 500 people gathered on the street to celebrate the turn of the century.

CHAPTER FIVE

Seeing the Woods, not the Trees

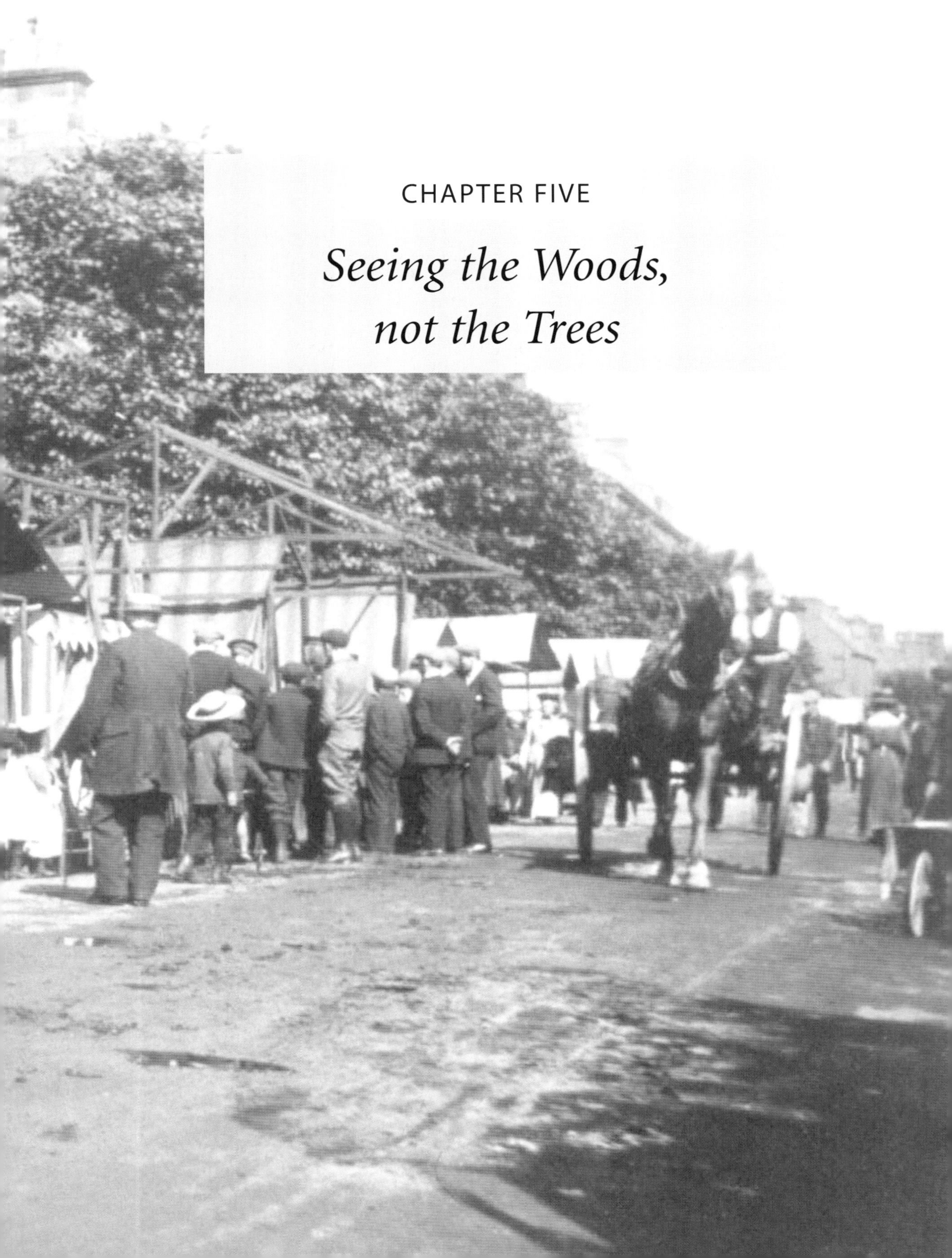

ST ANDREWS CASTLE 2005 ZZZ03915 (Shelagh Young)

CHANGE, IT IS SAID, is inevitable. Even the ancient castle is under attack again, this time from the sea. The 21st century is presenting challenges that cannot be ignored easily. For example, at the 2000 Open Championships in St Andrews the golfing prodigy Tiger Woods won with a record 19 under par, sparking debates over whether the Old Course provided sufficient challenge to the best contemporary golfers. Action was obviously needed if St Andrews was to retain its leading place in the global game of golf. Stewards of the Old Course have risen to the challenge. In 2005 the Royal and Ancient Club's Chief Executive Peter Dawson announced that the Old Course was being 'restored'. This was to ensure that traditional hazards would provide sufficient challenge to the extremely fit and well-equipped players taking part in the 2005 Open set to take place that July.

THE ROYAL AND ANCIENT CLUBHOUSE 2005
ZZZ03927 (Shelagh Young)

This was not the only significant change taking place as this book was being written. For example, £1.5 million was being spent on improving the Bruce Embankment, the sea defences originally sponsored by local philanthropist George Bruce in the 19th century, and the main access road to the West

Sands. The work is the responsibility of a steering group made up of staff from Fife Council, Scottish Enterprise Fife, the Royal and Ancient Golf Club and the St Andrews Links Trust.

Meanwhile, a tense debate was raging over the fate of the 126-year-old lime trees on South Street. Plans to chop them down and provide wider pavements as part of a £750,000 improvement scheme have enraged many residents. Local authority planners pointed to the damage done by the roots of trees that have outgrown their situation; they asked residents to transfer their affections to the proposed replacement trees, which would be expertly planted to avoid such problems in future. But not all residents were reassured, and some even threatened to stop any chainsaw-wielding operatives in their tracks.

Even a proposal to return to the old style parallel parking in North, South and Market Streets in place of the allegedly more dangerous diagonal parking has been interpreted as an example of the local authority disregarding the needs of residents. As anyone who has ever driven at a snail's place through St Andrews on a busy summer weekend in search of a parking place will tell you, traffic congestion is a growing problem. As in so many towns, the pressure on limited parking space is always a subject which seems capable of sparking anger in even the most mild-mannered resident.

For those who are least happy about the town's current development trajectory, the enemy, if there is one, seems to be the

SOUTH STREET 2005 ZZZ03930 (Shelagh Young)

AIKMAN & TERRAS ADVERTISEMENT C1930
ZZZ03947 (Courtesy of Norman Black)

A new series of mini roundabouts and pedestrian crossings have been blamed for some of today's traffic problems. The corner shop in the shadow of the disputed lime trees was once the premises of grocers Aikman & Terras. You can see from the old advertisement that the shop front is little changed.

partnership behind a re-branding exercise which came up with 'St Andrews World Class' as a new label for the erstwhile 'home of golf'. The partnership, which includes Fife Council, Fife Enterprise, St Andrews Tourist Board, St Andrews Bay Hotel, and the university, have been accused of putting tourists before taxpayers. It seems that some St Andreans feel that their town is being treated like a cash cow to be milked dry for the benefit of the country as a whole and at the expense of local residents. There are signs that this once tight-knit community no longer feels in control of its own destiny.

In response to criticism, the partnership has pointed to the annual £50 million generated by tourism and the needs of an estimated 700,000 annual visitors in terms of access, accommodation, parking and leisure facilities. Those who are implacably opposed to boosting tourist numbers find themselves pitted against formidable combined forces which include those very institutions that have helped to create this oasis of prosperity in a region in which the local economy has been struggling for many years.

Take the university, for example. While golf will undoubtedly continue to keep St Andrews on the leisure industry map, the place is also sustained in large part by its significant trade in knowledge. The university is generally credited with being the real engine of growth in the town. As one St Andrean put it, 'we don't actually make anything here any more, but we certainly know how to make people think.'

As the university itself boasts, its staff and students make up a third of the local population, but many more than that benefit from its influence. In my research I lost count of the number of people who called themselves lucky and declared themselves to be delighted to attend events such as the annual Stanza poetry festival as well as concerts, talks and seminars which they believe would not take place if it were not for the university. It is not that all such events are either hosted or paid for by the university, rather that the institution exerts a sort of cultural gravitational pull which helps sustain the arts, intellectual debate and music.

Did you know?

Red gowns are no longer worn every day by students, but you can still catch the occasional flash of red gown in town. The traditional Sunday pier walk continues after chapel whenever the pier is not closed for repairs.

THE SUNDAY PIER WALK 1982
SA000491 (Courtesy of University of St Andrews Library)

The university has an influence far beyond this small corner of Fife. For example, the opinion of its academics in the Centre for the Study of Terrorism and Political Violence is frequently sought by journalists and policymakers, and the university has forged many successful partnerships with other institutions and with businesses in the UK and abroad. Former members of staff jokingly refer to St Andrews as the academic's graveyard.

It seems that one certainly does not have to be a native-born St Andrean to experience something of its magnetic powers. Many people who come here to work decide to stay, and some continue to make great contributions in so-called retirement. Dr John Frew, now retired from the university, finds himself permanently caught up in debates about good and not so good development. If it were not for his work (and that of many of his students) on the built environment of St Andrews, there would not be such a rich resource to draw upon when fighting to preserve the look and feel of the town.

THE ST ANDREWS PRESERVATION TRUST MUSEUM, NORTH STREET 2005 ZZZ03929 (Shelagh Young)

A ST ANDREWS PRESERVATION TRUST SIGN 2005
ZZZ03914 (Shelagh Young)

LOUDENS CLOSE 2005 ZZZ03923 (Shelagh Young)

Thanks to the work of the St Andrews Preservation Trust, many of the fascinating ancient alleys, known as wynds, survived attempts at slum clearance. Loudens Close takes you down to the Lade Braes past a delightful row of old whitewashed cottages.

But preservation of buildings and environment are nothing if people do not feel they can also protect a valued way of life. Nearly every St Andrean I met while researching this book placed the high cost of housing near or at the top of a list of issues that concerned them. The fact is that between the twin pressures of well-heeled parents and enterprising landlords buying homes for student occupation and of retirees' dreams of a new life by the sea, many local young people can no longer afford to stay in the area. It is common to find that the people caring for the town's elderly, staffing the golf facilities, and filling lower-paid roles at the university now live elsewhere.

Some people believe that this signals a need for more affordable, possibly social, housing to be built in the town. Others are deeply opposed to any further significant building in and around the town. One resident pointed out that St Andrews would be a very dull place if everyone agreed about everything; others fear that the anti-development lobby will suffocate the town. For some, the St Andrews Preservation Trust-backed proposal for a protective green belt to completely restrict creeping suburbanisation is comforting. For others, the green belt looks more like a noose. However, we all know what 'housing development' usually means today. Unless someone at the local planning authority can be persuaded to take a radical stance, 'ticky tacky boxes', as one St Andrean grimly described them, sprout up like weeds on whatever land is made available.

SUPER STUDENT HOUSE TO RENT 2005
ZZZ03910 (Shelagh Young)

It does not look 'super'. Rents are high and housing expensive, even when the property is in poor condition.

Fortunately, St Andrews is brimful of challenging minds. The sharpest brains in the place are unwilling to allow the town to become stuck in the debate between the conservationists and the pro-development movement. John Di Folco, Chair of the Crawford Arts Centre, summed up the progressive view beautifully when he challenged me to think about Edinburgh's world-famous New Town. Built between 1776 and 1840, the plan of the town, designed by James Craig, was a stark contrast to the existing Old Town. There, buildings had grown over time, with floors added as the population grew. In comparison, the New Town plans seemed to celebrate uniformity. The streets were wide and designed in a simple grid pattern, the buildings were terraces of similar height and design. Now tourists praise its symmetry; but this was far from pleasing to the eye of all Edinburgh's citizens when the development was taking place. Some objected, but most were won over. Di Folco asks why such ambitious plans should be beyond us in the 21st century. Why not build a stunning new addition to St Andrews, one which complements rather than imitates or disregards its medieval heart?

In his role at the helm of the Crawford Arts Centre Board, which is currently based in North Street, Di Folco is clearly aligned with the progressives when it comes to development. A new purpose-built home for the centre is being proposed. It is intended to be modern in design, and to rub shoulders with the old museum building in Kinburn Park. Di Folco recognises that his organisation is in for a fight. Yet he has also supported the St Andrews Preservation Trust, and as a one-time member shares many of the concerns expressed by the trust regarding the fabric of the town. Di Folco was born in St Andrews, and has an obvious attachment to the place. To love the town, it seems, is not always to want to preserve every nook and cranny of it in aspic.

Golf promoters certainly have not helped to reassure St Andreans. Locals mutter darkly about the setting of dangerous planning precedents when new courses are granted limited planning permission for club buildings in formerly rural areas. If business slumps, will the developers push for failed golf courses to be transformed into land for housing? The spectacular collapse of a golf and leisure project which left the prominent new £9 million Gateway Building at the western entrance to the town standing empty for four years revealed that such economic disasters do happen. Despite its subsequent rescue by the university, the huge circular building stands as a reminder that speculative development is not yet a thing of the past, even in a town as loved, protected and successful as St Andrews.

It is not just tourism-related development that seems to inflame local sensibilities. For example, there have been objections to plans for a new health centre on the Largo Road, with some saying that its proposed position will make it too visible from the town and from approaches to the town, thus spoiling age-old views. A proposed new bus station is currently under critical scrutiny too. It often

THE GATEWAY BUILDING 2005 ZZZ03921 (Shelagh Young)

feels as if development plans are perceived as the tip of a dangerous iceberg threatening to wreck St Andrews as we know it, with consequences which as yet remain unseen.

This heated debate reveals the strength of feeling and the passion inspired in most people who spend any length of time in St Andrews. Living in St Andrews seems almost inevitably to lead to loving St Andrews, and for some that means keeping things just the way they are.

But is that good enough? At the controversial new Byre Theatre building in St Andrews, glass and polished steel meet rugged ancient stone walls in what many St Andreans proudly consider to be a stylish juxtaposition of old and new. Yet this building too was vehemently opposed at the planning stage. Sitting in the roomy café amid the conversational buzz and the promising clink of ice in tall glasses, many would find it hard to be anything other than energised by the prospect of growth and change in St Andrews. Even in the bleakest, coldest days of winter, the streets here have a vibrancy which is rare outside Britain's largest metropolitan centres. Despite losing its importance as a religious centre, St Andrews has rebuilt and maintained an international profile, firstly through golf, and latterly through the many achievements and connections forged under the auspices of the university.

There are signs too of a renewed interest in harnessing the energy of local people, and ensuring that St Andreans feel themselves to be at the heart rather than at the fringes of a new Scotland. For example, efforts are being made to turn St Andrews into one of Scotland's leading Fair Trade towns. Fair Trade goods, which ensure growers in the Third World get a fairer price for their products, are on sale in over 20 shops and cafes in St Andrews. Oxfam, which opened in Bell Street in 1971, leads the way with a range of over thirty Fair Trade food product lines, ranging from delicious bitter cocoa to chilli dry-roasted cashew nuts.

There is development in the arts too. In an exciting funding deal struck between Fife Council, the Scottish Arts Council, and the Crawford Arts Centre, St Andrews will become a focus for a wider ranging community arts programme for the whole of Fife. The decision to base the office of the Scottish Information Commissioner in St Andrews has also helped to increase the sense of St Andrews being an important player in the development of the new independent,

THE OFFICE OF THE SCOTTISH INFORMATION COMMISSIONER, KINBURN TERRACE 2005 ZZZ03905 (Shelagh Young)

Development at the Royal and Ancient

The rather archaic style of the Royal and Ancient Club, golf's governing body, has often been criticised. However, it is not just the Old Course that is changing to suit the needs of golfers in the new millennium. In the run up to the Royal and Ancient's 250th birthday in 2004, a historic decision was taken to allow women to participate in the decision-making process around the global governance of the game. The men-only club membership rule, which dates back to 1754, is unlikely to change in the near future, but it was announced in 2005 that women would no longer be barred from playing in the Open Championships. R & A secretary Peter Dawson was careful to say that women would not be competing with men in the Open Championships, leaving many confused as to just what exactly would result from a woman's application to play at the Open.

contemporary Scotland. These developments suggest an image that is wholly better suited to the abilities and spirit of its feisty residents than the heritage theme park image perpetrated by rather too many tourist brochures.

The decisions to allow women to play a role in golf's governing body and to enter the Open also reflected well on the community of St Andrews, with sports minister Richard Caborn, a keen golfer himself, saying that in making these changes 'the people of St Andrews are sending out a welcome message of inclusiveness and modernity.' No doubt some residents would disagree with this view; but whatever the actual position taken, a concern for ensuring that the best qualities of the place survive is what all St Andrean activists, armchair and otherwise, seem to share. Whatever perspective a contemporary St Andrean takes on the great development debate, or on any other issue affecting the future of their beloved town, they can always be confident that they will be part of an intelligent passionate, lively debate.

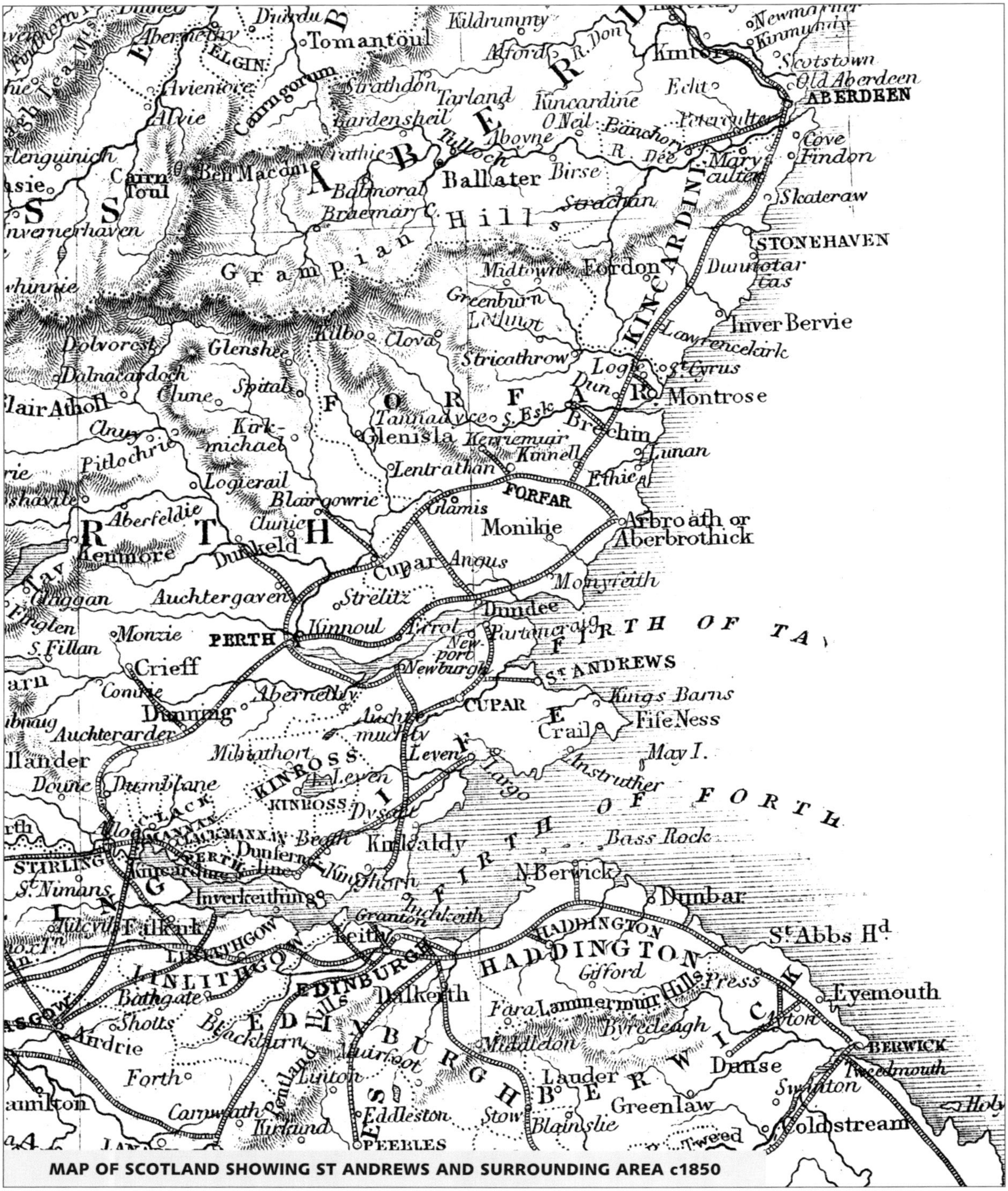

MAP OF SCOTLAND SHOWING ST ANDREWS AND SURROUNDING AREA c1850

Acknowledgements

The author wishes to thank all the staff and volunteers at the St Andrews Preservation Trust Museum and St Andrews University Library, as well as many residents of St Andrews, past and present, for their generous contributions to this book. These include curators Lesley and Rachel, and Cilla Jackson at the university, as well as Norman Black, Ann Cantley, Gordon Christie, Maryisa Denyer, John Di Folco, Dr John Frew, Pat Harvey and Betty Willsher. Authors whose work has been an invaluable source include Catherine Forrest, Raymond Lamont-Brown, David W Lyle, Catherine Pittaway and Betty Willsher. Thanks also to Cameron, Levi and Anthony for letting me get on with it.

I would also like to specifically thank the St Andrews Preservation Trust for allowing the use of items from their collection in this book.

Photographs used by courtesy of University of St Andrews Library are reproduced from digital copies of the originals held in the University of St Andrews Library. For further information about the collections, obtaining copies of images, or authorisation to reproduce them, please refer to http://specialcollections.st-and.ac.uk or contact Department of Special Collections, University of St Andrews Library, North Street, St Andrews, Fife KY16 9TR (tel 01334-462339); email speccoll@st-and.ac.uk

Further reading:

Raymond Lamont-Brown:
The Life and Times of St Andrews. John Donald Publishers Ltd, Edinburgh 1989

David W Lyle:
Shadows of St Andrews Past. John Donald Publishers Ltd, Edinburgh 1989

ed John Frew:
Building for a New Age. The Crawford Centre for the Arts (undated)

Betty Willsher:
St Andrews Citizens - Their Societies Past and Present. Librario Publishing Ltd, Kinloss 2003

Betty Willsher:
St Andrews – Ancient City in the Twentieth Century. Librario Publishing Ltd, Kinloss 2003

Ottakar's Bookshops

Ottakar's bookshops, the first of which opened in Brighton in 1988, can now be found in over 130 towns and cities across the United Kingdom. Expansion was gradual throughout the 1990s, but the chain has expanded rapidly in recent years, with many new shop openings and the acquisition of shops from James Thin and Hammicks.

Ottakar's has always known that a shop's local profile is as important, if not more important, than the chain's national profile, and has encouraged its staff to make their shops a part of the local community, tailoring stock to suit the area and forging links with local schools and businesses.

Local history has always been a strong area for Ottakar's, and the company has published its own award winning local history titles, based on text written by its customers, in recent years.

With a reputation for friendly, intelligent and enthusiastic booksellers, warm, inviting shops with an excellent range of books and related products, Ottakar's is now one of the UK's most popular booksellers. In 2003 and then again in 2004 it won the prestigious Best Bookselling Company of the Year Award at the British Book Awards.

Ottakar's has commissioned The Francis Frith Collection to create a series of town history books similar to this volume, as well as a range of stylish gift products, all illustrated with historical photographs.

Participating Ottakar's bookshops can be found in the following towns and cities:

Aberdeen
Abergavenny
Aberystwyth
Andover
Ashford
Ayr
Banbury
Barnstaple
Basildon
Berkhamsted
Bishop's Stortford
Boston
Brentwood
Bromley
Bury St Edmunds
Camberley
Canterbury
Carmarthen
Chatham
Chelmsford
Cheltenham
Cirencester
Coventry
Crawley
Darlington
Dorchester
Douglas, Isle of Man
Dumfries
Dundee
East Grinstead
Eastbourne
Elgin
Enfield
Epsom
Falkirk
Fareham
Farnham
Folkestone
Glasgow
Gloucester
Greenwich
Grimsby
Guildford
Harrogate
Hastings
Haywards Heath
Hemel Hempstead
High Wycombe
Horsham
Huddersfield
Inverness
Isle of Wight
Kendal
King's Lynn
Kirkcaldy
Lancaster
Lincoln
Llandudno
Loughborough
Lowestoft
Luton
Lymington
Maidenhead
Maidstone
Market Harborough
Milton Keynes
Newport
Newton Abbot
Norwich
Oban
Ormskirk
Petersfield
Portsmouth
Poole
Redhill
St Albans
St Andrews
St Neots
St Helier
Salisbury
Sheffield
Stafford
Staines
Stevenage
Sutton Coldfield
Teddington
Tenterden
Tiverton
Torquay
Trowbridge
Truro
Tunbridge Wells
Twickenham
Walsall
Wilmslow and Alderley Edge
Wells
Weston-super-Mare
Windsor
Witney
Woking
Worcester
Yeovil

Francis Frith

Pioneer Victorian Photographer

Francis Frith, founder of the world-famous photographic archive, was a complex and multi-talented man. A devout Quaker and a highly successful Victorian businessman, he was philosophical by nature and pioneering in outlook. By 1855 he had already established a wholesale grocery business in Liverpool, and sold it for the astonishing sum of £200,000, which is the equivalent today of over £15,000,000. Now in his thirties, and captivated by the new science of photography, Frith set out on a series of pioneering journeys up the Nile and to the Near East.

He was the first photographer to venture beyond the sixth cataract of the Nile. Africa was still the mysterious 'Dark Continent', and Stanley and Livingstone's historic meeting was a decade into the future. The conditions for picture taking confound belief. He laboured for hours in his wicker dark-room in the sweltering heat of the desert, while the volatile chemicals fizzed dangerously in their trays. Back in London he exhibited his photographs and was 'rapturously cheered' by members of the Royal Society. His reputation as a photographer was made overnight.

By the 1870s the railways had threaded their way across the country, and Bank Holidays and half-day Saturdays had been made obligatory by Act of Parliament. All of a sudden the working man and his family were able to enjoy days out, take holidays, and see a little more of the world.

With typical business acumen, Francis Frith foresaw that these new tourists would enjoy having souvenirs to commemorate their days out. For the next thirty years he travelled the country by train and by pony and trap, producing fine photographs of seaside resorts and beauty spots that were keenly bought by millions of Victorians. These prints were painstakingly pasted into family albums and pored over during the dark nights of winter, rekindling precious memories of summer excursions. Frith's studio was soon supplying retail shops all over the country, and by 1890 F Frith & Co had become the greatest specialist photographic publishing company in the world, with over 2,000 sales outlets, and pioneered the picture postcard.

Francis Frith had died in 1898 at his villa in Cannes, his great project still growing. By 1970 the archive he created contained over a third of a million pictures showing 7,000 British towns and villages.

Frith's legacy to us today is of immense significance and value, for the magnificent archive of evocative photographs he created provides a unique record of change in the cities, towns and villages throughout Britain over a century and more. Frith and his fellow studio photographers revisited locations many times down the years to update their views, compiling for us an enthralling and colourful pageant of British life and character.

We are fortunate that Frith was dedicated to recording the minutiae of everyday life. For it is this sheer wealth of visual data, the painstaking chronicle of changes in dress, transport, street layouts, buildings, housing and landscape that captivates us so much today, offering us a powerful link with the past and with the lives of our ancestors.

Computers have now made it possible for Frith's many thousands of images to be accessed almost instantly. The archive offers every one of us an opportunity to examine the places where we and our families have lived and worked down the years. Its images, depicting our shared past, are now bringing pleasure and enlightenment to millions around the world a century and more after his death. For further information visit: www.francisfrith.co.uk

FREE PRINT OF YOUR CHOICE

Mounted Print
Overall size 14 x 11 inches (355 x 280mm)

Choose any Frith photograph in this book.
Simply complete the Voucher opposite and return it with your remittance for £2.25 (to cover postage and handling) and we will print the photograph of your choice in SEPIA (size 11 x 8 inches) and supply it in a cream mount with a burgundy rule line (overall size 14 x 11 inches).
Please note: photographs with a reference number starting with a "Z" are not Frith photographs and cannot be supplied under this offer.
Offer valid for delivery to one UK address only.

***PLUS:* Order additional Mounted Prints at HALF PRICE - £7.49 each** (normally £14.99)
If you would like to order more Frith prints from this book, possibly as gifts for friends and family, you can buy them at half price (with no additional postage and handling costs).

***PLUS:* Have your Mounted Prints framed**
For an extra £14.95 per print you can have your mounted print(s) framed in an elegant polished wood and gilt moulding, overall size 16 x 13 inches (no additional postage and handling required).

IMPORTANT!

These special prices are only available if you use this form to order. You must use the ORIGINAL VOUCHER on this page (no copies permitted). We can only despatch to one UK address. This offer cannot be combined with any other offer.

Send completed Voucher form to:
The Francis Frith Collection, Frith's Barn, Teffont, Salisbury, Wiltshire SP3 5QP

CHOOSE A PHOTOGRAPH FROM THIS BOOK

Voucher *for FREE and Reduced Price Frith Prints*

Please do not photocopy this voucher. Only the original is valid, so please fill it in, cut it out and return it to us with your order.

Picture ref no	Page no	Qty	Mounted @ £7.49	Framed + £14.95	Total Cost £
		1	Free of charge*	£	£
			£7.49	£	£
			£7.49	£	£
			£7.49	£	£
			£7.49	£	£
			£7.49	£	£
			* Post & handling		£2.25
			Total Order Cost		£

Please allow 28 days for delivery.
Offer available to one UK address only

Title of this book ....
I enclose a cheque/postal order for £ ....
made payable to 'The Francis Frith Collection'

OR please debit my Mastercard / Visa / Maestro / Amex card, details below

Card Number

Issue No (Maestro only) Valid from (Maestro)

Expires Signature

Name Mr/Mrs/Ms ....
Address ....
....
....
.... Postcode ....
Daytime Tel No ....
Email ....

ISBN: 1-84567-753-6 Valid to 31/12/08